CRY WOLF! and LAUGH!

"Jack Douglas is a kook of the TV comic world who reports his surprise and distress in adjusting to 'Old New Litchridge' after living in Manhattan's canyons. The wolf of title is a family pet who is intimidated by the wild behavior of the Douglas neighbors.

Around the wolf problem Douglas scatters the usual suburban ones of drunken neighbors, capitalist plumbers, quaint local politicians, quaint storekeepers, quaint architecture, and brash children." *Buffalo Evening News*

THE GREAT HARDCOVER BESTSELLER IS NOW UNLEASHED ON THE UNSUSPECTING WORLD OF PAPERBACK READERS! BEWARE AND LAUGH!

The Neighbors Are Scaring My Wolf

Jack Douglas

AVON
PUBLISHERS OF
DISCUS • CAMELOT • BARD

AVON BOOKS
A division of
The Hearst Corporation
959 Eighth Avenue
New York, New York 10019

Published by arrangement with E. P. Dutton & Co., Inc.
Library of Congress Catalog Card Number: 68-25783.

First Avon Printing, October, 1969

Cover illustration by Roy Doty.

Printed in the U.S.A.

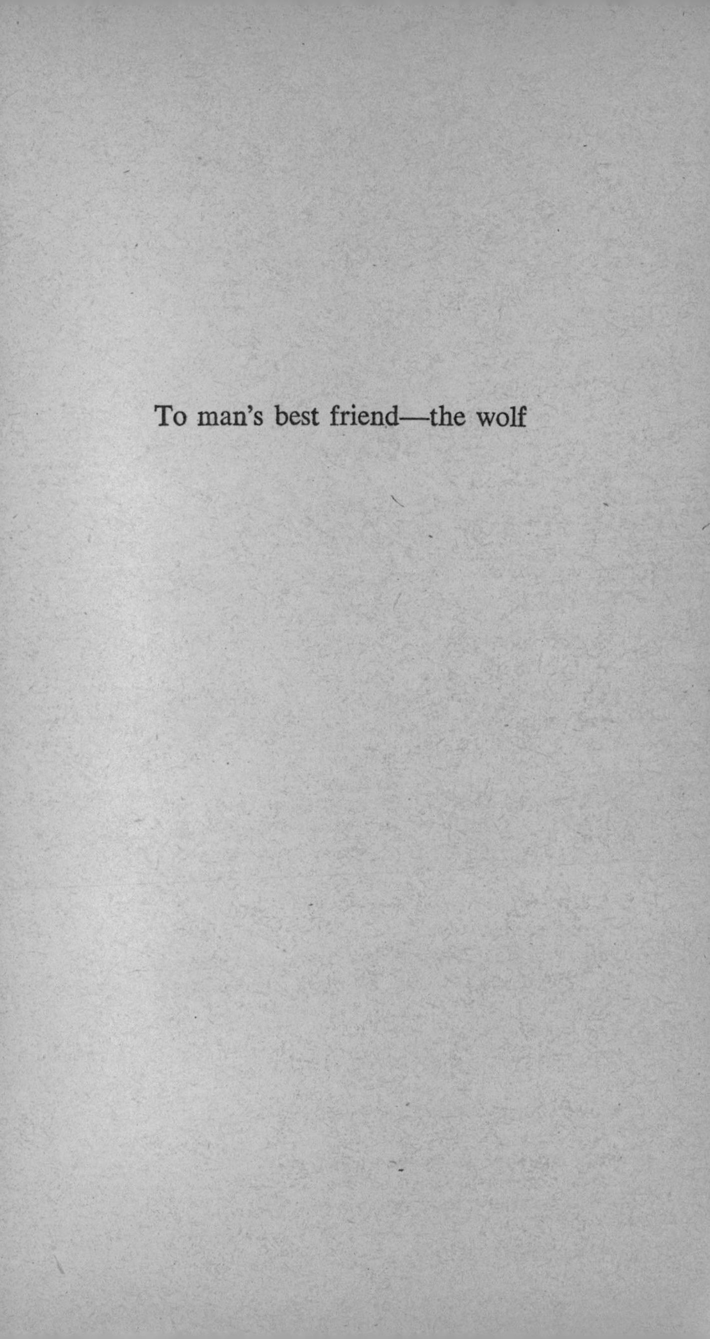

To man's best friend—the wolf

The Neighbors Are Scaring My Wolf

chapter 1

THE REASON WE MOVED FROM THE CITY to the Outer Suburbia community of Old New Litchridge in Connecticut was because Tony Randall likes the cheese store there. "Ask Jack Paar," he said to Reiko and me one night in Danny's Hideaway. "He *loves* the cheese store in Old New Litchridge. So do Paul Newman and Hubert Humphrey and Tempest Storm."

"I was thinking about something a bit farther away from New York," I said. "I've got my eye on a little place in Sioux Lookout, Montana."

"How do you know they have a cheese store there?" said Tony. "I mean—that everybody loves." That made sense, so the following Saturday we rented an unreliable car and drove up to Old New Litchridge to make the rounds of the local real-estate lairs.

The establishments we visited in this lovely little town seemed to hire their representatives from the same place that elephants go to die. I think what happens is—these genetic phenomena follow the elephants. Then, when they get there they change their minds and come back and start to sell real estate. Mostly, they are lovely blue-rinsed gentlewomen who have outlived their husbands and the saber-toothed cat by many years, and I'm sure they remember the Ice Age vividly.

Locally they are known as the Old New Litchridge Witches, and occasionally when one of them cheats a little and sells a charming saltbox for less than the agreed-upon larcenous 6 percent, she is shoved into a car trunk and driven up to Salem for burning. It can't be done in Old New Litchridge because the dampness makes them too hard to light.

We drew old Mrs. Putnam from the Borgia Realty Company's pool, and after I had guided her into her station wagon and put her foot on the gas pedal, she said, "I'm Mrs. Putnam. I'm a direct descendant of General Israel Putnam who was the commander in chief of the Continental Army during the Revolutionary War."

"I've read about him," I said neutrally.

"Yes," she said. "It was all in the papers. Now—what would you like to see? The park? We have a lovely park. Beautiful pond there. Ducks swim there all the time. Beautiful pond. You should see it in the wintertime. It's just like a picture by Currier and Ives—not many people drown."

"That's nice to know," I said.

"What's Currier and Ives?" said Reiko.

"Mrs. Putnam," I said, "we'd like to buy a house here in Old New Litchridge."

"You should see it in the wintertime," said Mrs. Putnam. "It's just like Currier and Ives."

Old Mrs. Putnam finally showed us several houses, and her approach to our problem was the same at every house, and was no different from any other real-estate agent's I have met down through the years. As they drive you into the driveway of the house they wish to dump on you, they make it sound as though you've just taken possession—through the magic of osmosis, or the Time Tunnel, or Alice-Baby's looking glass. From the first ecstatic (they try to make it seem) view, it's: "Now here's your lovely driveway—lined with your beautiful poplars and your lovely velvety green lawn. And there's your lovely old colonial house, with your lovely chimneys and your lovely windows and your lovely front door—and your lovely door knocker. Give a lovely knock on your lovely door with your lovely door knocker." You do—and after all this premature possessiveness, it gives you a real jolt when two perfect strangers answer your lovely door. What the hell are *they* doing in *your* house!!!!!

After each house which we didn't like, Mrs. Putnam said, "You should see it in the wintertime. It's just like Currier and Ives."

"Maybe we ought to come back in January," I said.

Mrs. Putnam smiled her Mona Lisa smile, making her look like a retired snake, and drove on. After some hours, I said, "Have you got anything in Sioux Lookout, Montana?"

"How many bedrooms?" said Mrs. Putnam. I knew right then we'd never leave that station wagon alive unless we bought a house from Old Mrs. Putnam—in Old New Litchridge.

Finally, as we were approaching the desperation stage, which I'm sure Old Mrs. Putnam was counting on, she played her trump card. "I have one more place," she said, "but I'm not sure they want to sell—" Immediately I was on my knees—begging, pleading, promising anything. A place that somebody doesn't want to sell is just what everybody wants! It was what *I* wanted!

The place was lovely. Much to our delight it was situated on what was actually an island. It was surrounded on all sides by water—two streams and a willow-lined pond—and was approached over a small stone bridge. The style of the house was "contemporary," which bore Mrs. Putnam out, and it had tremendous plate-glass windows which didn't do much for privacy, but the view across the surrounding meadows and wooded hills was breathtaking. The living room had an enormous fireplace, and the master bathroom had a sunken blue-tiled bathtub. I quickly conjured up two images in my mind. One, lolling for hours up to my ears in bubble bath bubbles in this enchanting blue bathtub; the other, lolling for hours, toasting myself in front of a huge log fire in the living room, while lovely white snow fell softly outside the large picture windows. I should have conjured up a third image of the lovely large white mortgage, but I didn't. I just wrote a very substantial check, and Old Mrs. Putnam, through some miracle, persuaded the owners to take it. At last—we had a home in Old New Litchridge.

On the way back to the real-estate office, I asked Mrs. Putnam about the cheese store.

"Oh, he closed up last week and went out West somewhere—and opened up a new store," she said.

This was a blow. "Where—out West?"

"It's just a small town in Montana—strange name for a town—Sioux Lookout."

"Mommie?" said Bobby, sleepily. "What's Currier and Ives?"

"Papa knows," said Reiko, holding Bobby tighter.

chapter 2

WHEN YOU BUY A HOME IN THE SUBURBS, there are three inevitables which you must accustom yourself to. The mortgage. The taxes. And the neighbors.

The mortgage is something which you pay off in monthly installments. The last installment becomes due just before the dinosaurs take over again.

Taxes you will always have, because taxes are needed to build schools so that the future generation may learn that education isn't everything.

So much has been written about neighbors who irritate, annoy, and enrage that I feel I should write a few kind words in the *defense* of neighbors, but after going through the list of people who live around us, I have decided against it. Besides—the neighbors are scaring my wolf.

About two years ago Reiko was driving along Jones Ridge Road on her way to the A & P, when she was forced off the road and into a large rock by a wildly careening Mayflower moving van—the driver of which had apparently been totally unprepared for Dead Man's Hill and Suicide Bend.

A few minutes later the Poor Butterfly was back home with her frightened story and two front tires that needed an emergency herniotomy. By an ominous coincidence the Mayflower van had pulled up in front of the empty house next door and was already being unloaded. This was our introduction (and though we did not know it then, the shadow of things to come) to our new neighbors—a quasi-divorcee, Mrs. Charles Kloompt, rumored to be a former Transylvanian countess, her son Chuckie, aged five, a butler, Max, and a West Indian nurse, who looked like a hassock.

The first thing this Mrs. Kloompt did was have the diving board removed from her newly acquired swimming pool and have it thrown across the little brook that separates *her* four acres from *our* two, so her Chuckie could cross the water without getting his twenty-dollar loafers wet when he wished to play with our peasant-child, Bobby. A man's home is his castle, but this surprise bridging of our moat gave me the uneasy feeling that some morning I would awaken to find a huge wooden horse on the other side of the brook.

As the day wore on it grew more interesting—for me. My office faces the meadow in back of our new neighbor's house, and from time to time the steamy brutes of Mayflower carried large concrete statues into the open field and set them upright. From my forward observation post, all of these concrete statues looked as if they had been uprooted from the palace at Versailles, where I'm sure they didn't clash with the rest of the Versailles decor, as they did in their present location. A Connecticut meadow is no place for concrete nymphs, satyrs, and Louie the Fourteenth. At twilight or on an early misty morning, it looked like a *National Geographic* view of Easter Island. Or a cemetery for queers.

As inartistic as I felt this nutty statuary to be, it had its practical side. A sneak thief dashing across these fields in the dark after snatching a TV set from the house could get the shock of his life in two ways —he could feel that he had been surrounded by vigilantes or he could accidentally smash into one of the statues and not only ruin his recent acquisition but have his front teeth rearranged.

These statues also proved the undoing of my writer friend, Herb Cameron. Herb had been riding his horse across these fields for fifteen years and never had there been any problem until Mrs. Kloompt took over. Herb took the concrete obstacles as well as could be expected, but his old horse, Jerry, shied south about twenty feet, leaving Herb suspended in midair for three seconds, which gave him plenty of time to run through his complete catalog of obscenity and recite a short Hindu prayer before he crashed down into a jolly pile of recently digested oats. Poor Herb was a mess. I made him stand outside while I prepared a pitcher of extra dry Martinis, which he drank *downwind*. He may never "Tallyho" again.

The first time we saw our new neighbor she was dressed in a bikini and wandering up and down the brook. Every once in a while she would stop and feel around the bottom with her bare foot. Then she would pose, so she thought, *provocatively*. I felt that maybe I should get out my sheepskin slacks and my cloven hooves and chase her around a bit. This was what seemed to be expected. Before I had a chance to decide whether to be a good neighbor or a satyr, she gave up and clumped back to the house, her bikinied hips swaying like the rear end of a retreating duck with one short leg. Right then and there I decided that *here* was a neighbor who most certainly marched to a different drum.

We soon learned much more than we cared to know about this new group. Mrs. Kloompt, or Olenka as she begged us to call her, was extremely witty, entertaining, fascinating, charming, and gracious—for the first fifteen or twenty minutes after we met that night at dinner. After that she started to repeat her entertaining bon mots. And smoke a cigar. Her charm and graciousness vanished after she slapped the butler's face a few times because the wine was too warm—or too cold—or too just right. And her fascination evaporated with her monologue about her hatred of her mother. Mother hatred doesn't bother me—so long as it's done well—but Madame Kloompt had no finesse at all. Her mother, who wasn't allowed to eat with the guests, was out in the kitchen putting Mercurochrome on the butler's lower jaw, but I'm sure she could hear every word her witty, entertaining, fascinating, charming, and gracious daughter was saying about her—the principal witty, entertaining, fascinating, charming, and gracious scoop (confided in a shout) was that her dear mother was *insane!*

The need for public confession seemed to be an old family custom with this group, because later, in the secret confines of the guest powder room, the mother whispered to Reiko that she mustn't pay any attention to what her witty, entertaining, fascinating, charming, and gracious daughter said because she was mentally deranged and hadn't been taking her shock treatments lately.

The other guests at this festive first night in Old New Litchridge were Randolf Romanoff, a writer, who was supposed to be one of *the* Romanoffs, who escaped the shooting that long-ago dark night in that Russian subcellar. (They must have had a large bus waiting outside that night.) This Romanoff was quite vague about what he had written, and when we first met he extended his hand with the fingers hanging down limply. I had to fight it, but I didn't kiss his jade fingertips.

Another guest was a King who will have to be anonymous, in print, because I have no wish to embarrass him or the country he is exiled from. The King, whom his small entourage rightfully addressed as "Your Highness," looked, Reiko confided later, like Phil Silvers. And I understand because of the enforced separation from his native land and its more or less well filled coffers, this King now works for a Texas savings and loan company. His Highness had very little to say at dinner, principally because "Madame" never closed her mouth once. She used one side of it for chewing and the other for expounding on a variety of subjects—of which she had not the slightest knowledge. I could not bring myself to address the King as "Your Highness" until it was time to leave, and then when I said "Good night, Your Highness," I felt like I was in my high-school play.

As the days stretched into weeks and months, we grew less and less intimate with Mrs. Kloompt. And as the days stretched into weeks and months, it became apparent that *everyone* had grown less intimate with Mrs. Kloompt. Except the butler, who seemed immune to both physical and oral abuse. The servants—nurses, extra butlers, gardeners, chauffeurs, etc.—appeared to be using Mrs. Kloompt's ménage as a way station to better things. We used to watch every morning to see what form Chuckie's nurse would assume that day. They were all shapes and colors and temperaments. Some of them would leave the first hour. Others would last past lunch. Very few made it to dinner. Mrs. Kloompt felt that a child's nurse should take on a few *other* small tasks such as raking leaves, shoveling snow, and maybe removing a dead tree or two. The commands to perform these extracurricular duties were given in a voice slightly louder than Hitler addressing Mussolini by long-distance phone when things weren't going too well. Soon, most of the world supply of domestic help had been depleted by this unpleasable vixen. The last was a maid from South America, who I thought was going to work out fine, but she turned out to be Martin Bormann, who decided after a few rounds with Madame that the South American jungle, with its boa constrictors and poison dart blowers, was a lot more pleasant than Fairfield County under Attila the Hun's older sister.

Before Mrs. Kloompt and the gypsy camp moved in next door, my wolf—whom I've had since he was a tiny puppy and had lovingly raised into a thoroughly domesticated and affectionate animal—was well adjusted to the stresses and strains of civilization. Being an extremely large timber wolf, he was also fearless until Mrs. Kloompt arrived, and next door became a Zulu kraal. Now he's a nervous, wild-eyed, collapsible wreck. All because of Madame's stainless-steel, piano-wire vocal chords. Her patio telephone is two hundred feet away from the wolf's pen and our bedroom window, but it doesn't seem so when she is trying to complete one of her numerous calls to Europe, during which she invariably gets cut off. This brings on a screaming avalanche of colorful Transylvanian epithets directed at the telephone company in Prague or Paris or Baden-Baden. If some simple long-distance operator stumbles into the trap of trying to reason with her, this sends her into a combination epileptic fit, stroke, convulsion, and screaming rabies! Once, during one of these ear-piercing maledictions, her voice reached such an awesome pitch she killed a whole field of daisies.

These telephone nightmares, plus the daily routine of screeching commands and orders to her flailed flock, helped to break down my wolf.

There are no wolf psychiatrists, so *I* have to give him an hour a day, during which time I try to explain that people aren't as nice as wolves. I lay his beautiful silver-gray head on my lap and try to soothe away the fear and bewilderment in his lovely amber eyes. I say softly, over and over again, "Trust us. We love you." But every time I get him calmed down, the voice of doom laser-beams across the brook and he faints. Then it's murder! Have you ever tried giving a full-grown wolf mouth-to-mouth resuscitation? It's like being dropped from a helicopter into a Grand Canyon of teeth.

Lately, he seems more able to cope—so now every time the Banshee of Bucharest starts shrieking, he just dives into a little bomb shelter I have made for him and there he stays until the all clear (actually it is never all clear unless she has gone back to New York for a few days or she has lost her voice—a miracle which has happened only once when she accidentally fell down with an LSD lollipop in her mouth).

Madame Kloompt and I are no longer speaking. Not because she kept scaring hell out of my wolf, but because of a simple, God-sent misunderstanding.

Madame Kloompt and some of her weirdo guests thought conditions were ideal for a bonfire on the driest and windiest night of the year.

We were speechless with terror when we saw what the Czarina and what looked like the cast of *Midsummer Night's Dream* were doing. The flames were high enough to start devouring some of the upper branches of a clump of defenseless birch trees that had unfortunately picked this unpremeditated disaster area to grow in. But the flames were not high enough to satisfy these not-so-latent fire worshipers. They got cans of gasoline and cleaning fluid and ether and started pouring their contents on the holocaust—right out of the *can!*

"Holy self-immolation!" said Bobby, fresh from an educational TV program.

The fire was now rapidly approaching the time when the surrounding countryside should be warned to prepare for evacuation, and at the same time, fly in a few forest-fire-wise Apache Indians from Gallup. Suddenly it was all over. The Old New Litchridge Fire Department, with its hundreds of eager volunteers, sirened onto the scene and doused the conflagration.

Exactly three moments later, the pyromaniac was on the telephone to me. I couldn't see her but I knew she was flecked with froth. She was that angry. I picked out a phrase here and there and found that she was accusing me of calling the fire department and also the police, who were there now. It was useless to try to tell her that we had nothing to do with it, so after giving her enough time to have one or two good orgasms, I hung up.

As the fire department and the police left, she screamed after them that as soon as they got out of sight she would build the biggest goddamn sonofabitchin' bonfire the world has ever seen. She made it sound like another Rome, and it damn near was.

This second fire made the first fire look like baby's first birthday cake. The flames consumed the innocent birch trees entirely, as she heaped tons of dead branches and leaves and anything else she thought might be combustible. She was alone now and in a blind fury, and when she ran out of fuel, she burned three-quarters of her porch furniture. All the time, she kept shrieking across the brook in the direction of our house, "Sonsabitches! Insane sonsabitches!" Then finally, "Insane *Hollywood* sonsabitches!" Which I thought was just the right touch.

Suddenly she stopped feeding the fire and looked at her depleted porch, then she turned and walked down to the edge of the brook—cupped her hands—and screamed with great dignity, "Why should I waste my porch furniture on you insane sonsabitches!!!"

Then she walked back into the house and lit a cigar.

To the east of us we have a lovely couple with seven children. All boys and known in the neighborhood as the Purple Gang. These people have a sign in their driveway warning *dogs*. This couple are very happy, carefree, and gay—on weekends. During the week it's *Wuthering Heights* with a dash of *Dial M for Murder*. He gets off the train at "The Next Station to Paradise" which is what Old New Litchridge is known as. I don't know where this tricky little slogan came from, but I have an idea. Old New Litchridge is on a wickedly sharp curve and someday the train won't make it and the slogan will come abruptly true. I feel that down deep "The Next Station to Paradise" is part of the death wish felt by everybody who has to ride this train. But let's get back to the couple next door. They're more fun than a barrel of turned-on monkeys. Charlie (that's *his* name) gets off the 5:09 from Grand Central and shuffles silently to the waiting car. He gets in and slams the door. He doesn't say one word to his wife, because he has had a *bad day* at the *office*. He has had a bad day at the office every day for twenty years. He has tried to ease the pain and unfulfillment in the bar car of the New Haven, but it doesn't work. It never has worked. As he alights at the station, any slight stimulation and false warmth he has picked up along the rickety-rockety route from the bright lights of Fun City to the pastoral pleasures of Outer Suburbia evaporate as soon as he sees his wife at the wheel of his battered station wagon, with its heavy starboard list caused by four yelping dogs and one screaming child. None of whom is glad to see him. They're just hungry.

Charlie's wife Madge tries to make conversation on the five-minute drive to their house, but even if Charlie felt up to it, the bedlam created by the dogs and child would preclude anything but a numb nod. Charlie likes dogs but I'm sure he often wishes he had thought twice about Great Danes and standard French poodles. And children.

When Charlie and Madge get home, Charlie makes himself a pot of Martinis while Madge alternately judo-chops the older children and drains the spaghetti.

Charlie never eats with the family. He has to *unwind* a little after the torture he has undergone all day at the "shop." He turns on the television set and then sits staring at the growing mound that houses his indigestion. When the police arrive to question his sons about the latest mailbox destructions and cherry bombings, he acknowledges their presence by breaking wind. They bow and continue their investigation.

At 11:00 P.M. Charlie decides he's hungry and whips up a cheese soufflé, then heads for his bed, a destination at which he seldom arrives. Madge usually finds him either on the living-room couch or inside their baby grand piano, which he mistakes for his mother's womb. Apparently his mother was quite musical and accessible.

In the morning the whole process is reversed. Charlie gets up and has two Bloody Marys (with real blood), and Madge drives him down to catch the 7:38. Charlie kisses the station wagon good-bye and crawls up the train steps—and thus begins another day in the intriguing world of big business.

On weekends the whole picture changes. Charlie is bright and cheery and smiling and zesty. He has a good word for the whole wide world because this is *Saturday* and Saturday is *fun day!* First to zoom around his two acres astride his Mighty Midget grass cutter and snowblower! Ah, to smell the newly spread steer manure! Makes a man glad to be alive! The hills are alive with the sound of music! And in no time at all it will be the *cocktail hour!* The life of a country squire seems sweet indeed!

After performing a delicate hysterectomy on a knot-hole in an ancient elm tree with a dull auger, he changes into something more country squirish. Red velvet loafers, beige corduroy slacks, and a Mexican wedding shirt. Fellow country squires and their wenches arrive and the beginning of Saturday night is under way.

Gin and vodka Martinis are the "in" drink. Ten parts gin and ten parts vodka. On Saturday night the vermouth is flown over Old New Litchridge by a low-flying crop duster. The cocktails are strong in this part of the country, and for good reason—it takes more than natural courage to face the large bowl of chopped clam dip.

Some people stop by for just *one* drink and stay until noon the next day.

By 6:30 the party is swinging, Charlie is Joe the Bartender, Dale Carnegie, and Hubert Humphrey all rolled into one big ball of conviviality and congeniality. He is witty. He is jovial. He is sweet and kind and reverent and loyal and trustworthy and smashed. The world is his tonight! The hills are alive with the sound of music!

This same rosy aura hovers over Charlie's and Madge's all day Sunday as people drop by for drinks and conversation and earnest discussions about what to do about hairy aphids and what to feed cardinals (the bird). I walk my animals, Chibi and Tanuki, across their field and Charlie waves gaily. Then Charlie waves gaily at the Boston–New York 727 jet overhead. He likes to think they dip their wings when they see him. He likes to think the pilot announces over the loudspeaker to the passengers: "If you look below to the left, you'll see good old Charlie Dawson waving gaily, which means we'll be landing at LaGuardia in three minutes."

As the long bright afternoon dissolves into the Twilight Zone, Charlie's fiery glow turns to clammy ashes. Tomorrow is Monday. The Day They Shot Lincoln. The Day They Stabbed Caesar. The Day They Hanged Nathan Hale. And the Day the Beatles Made Their First Recording. Gradually as the evening inexorably grinds toward the Ed Sullivan Show, Charlie's multiloquence decreases and finally stops altogether, except for a few Neanderthal grunts. The guests, recognizing the signs of decaying hospitality, wisely shout their good-byes from the driveway, and zoom off to safer surroundings. And Charlie and Madge are alone. Madge is much more alone than Charlie, because Charlie always has his indigestion, which is the only living thing he isn't mad at (or that isn't mad at him).

Another neighbor is the squirrel assassin. A retired bologna manufacturer, he apparently had concealed a boyhood ambition to be a sniper all through his life, until now, when he is wealthy enough to indulge himself. He spends most of his waking hours crouched on the back patio of his brick Normandy house.

This kindly soul is up in the morning before the squirrels so he can bait the target area with cracked corn, bread crumbs, and sunflower seeds. This execution ground is a little less than eighteen feet from the place where the long black snout of his custom-built .50-calibre Griffin & Howe rifle pokes through the plastic eel grass and palm frond blind—always at the ready. This "sportsman," as he is categorized on the social pages of the Old New Litchridge *Advertiser*, splatters six or seven squirrels a day. At night, with a special German-made infrared scope, he ambushes about the same number of field mice, whose heads—when he can find them—he has mounted on matchbox covers and hung on the wall of his trophy room.

Irving Greenthumb is another neighbor. That really isn't his name but it should be. Irving and his wife Carol are in love—not with each other but with their immaculate garden. They are up in the morning at dawn—watering, fertilizing, pruning, spraying, transplanting, and praying. They're praying because no matter how much they water, fertilize, prune, spray, and transplant—nothing grows. Irving and Carol are the black death so far as Mother Nature is concerned. Every year they sow a Garden of Eden and reap a dust bowl. But they don't give up. At their nagging insistence, an expert horticulturist from the State of Connecticut Department of Agriculture visited their cultivated pesthole. He tested their dirt for nematodes. Then he tested their nematodes for dirt. They were *pretty dirty*. That was his diagnosis.

Irving and Carol are so sensitive to the likes and dislikes of the plant world they have one Du Pont insecticide factory working nights. Everything that moves is sprayed, including a Gristede's delivery boy, who had to be rushed to a decompression chamber after he had inadvertently passed under a rose arbor which was being saturation bombed with Black Flag.

"That's one of the reasons Gristede's is expensive," explained Herb Cameron. "Decompression chambers run high."

Irving and Carol Greenthumb don't garden anymore. Their fervent enthusiasm died with their LBJ rosebush. The LBJ rose was a hybrid—a cross between a Teddy Roosevelt floribunda and a Mamie Van Doren polyantha—and came from California by special registered mail. It could not be flown because of its sensitivity to height. This, Irving and Carol learned when the tiny rosebush arrived. The information brought them to the verge of twin nervous breakdowns, because *their* rose garden was on a slight hill. The rosebush was immediately taken by Davey Tree Surgery ambulance to sea level at Westport, and the slight hill was bulldozed down to a more salubrious altitude. Then the precious rosebush was returned by easy stages. And under observation all the way by a battery of Dr. Davey's rose internes. The LBJ rose made the trip without any serious consequences and was finally planted in the newly lowered hill. After the joyful interment, the Davey Tree Surgery quartet sang "Oh, What a Beautiful Morning," and a medley of lesser Rodgers and Hammerstein hymns, while Irving and Carol stood, hand in hand, at the edge of this now hallowed ground, tears of happiness running down their cheeks. It was spring and the warm sun shone down on the new little rosebush and it seemed quite content with its new home, the Connecticut fertilizer, and Irving and Carol.

Late that afternoon, as the sun started to go down behind the fresh budding oaks and sycamores, Irving suddenly screamed. Carol sprang from her bubble bath where she had been soaking off topsoil and ran stark naked into the garden, where Irving was standing like a man possessed, pointing at the sky. Carol looked up and saw—to her unbelieving horror—an immense flock of Canada geese flying *south!!!* "No! No! No! It's not true!" Carol moaned. "It's spring! It said so right in the garden section of *The New York Times!*"

Irving got himself under control and dashed madly around checking each one of his thirty-six thermometers. Then he quickly averaged them up. It *was* getting colder. Fast. Irving with Carol, still naked, started to dig up the LBJ rosebush. A minor New York Mafia member, driving by with his family, said to his wife, "Ya see, Gertrude—that's what I mean when I say Fairfield County is no place to bring up kids!"

Irving and Carol got the delicate rosebush into the house, knowing full well that what they did during the next few hours could mean life or death. They knew the temperature must be controlled without variance. Carol felt there was only one way to do this, so she removed a half-roasted capon from the oven, dropping a few half-baked potatoes that rolled around the kitchen floor. Then they gently eased the rosebush into the oven (the *lower* shelf).

Irving and Carol stood separate watches that night as the outside temperature dropped at an alarming rate. They didn't know it, but Connecticut was at the beginning of the coldest spring they had had since spring the year before.

Irving took a sabbatical from his job as vice-president of the Big Brownie Cookie Company and devoted all of his waking hours and quite a few of his sleeping hours to the preservation of the LBJ rosebush. Carol lived on tranquilizers and wake-up pills and never answered when spoken to.

Herb Cameron dropped by one day during the crisis and came away reporting that they were acting like Monsieur and Madame Curie on the eve of discovering radium.

Irving and Carol knew that the rosebush needed sunshine to keep it alive, but it also needed warmth. It was still too cold to put the bush outside, so they tried a sunlamp. Irving and Carol got brown as berries, but the rosebush's buds started to turn gray. Irving and Carol thought of a transfusion. But who did they know with rose blood?

The LBJ rosebush was fading fast. Irving and Carol could not help it more. Irving finally said, "Why don't we take it outside and plant it where it was planted before—at least if it dies, it will be in the soil it loves, and surrounded by the lovely Connecticut countryside. Maybe that will ease the pain." Carol agreed, and they chopped a hole through the icy soil and planted the LBJ rosebush facing the east, where, please God, it would live to see another sunrise.

The LBJ rosebush saw many, many other sunrises and grew into a huge, lovely, and vigorous plant—covered with hundreds of beautiful pink and peach-colored roses.

In the fall of that year Irving ordered five tons of crushed stone for the driveway. The five tons of crushed stone arrived one morning before Irving and Carol were up, so the driver of the crushed stone truck very carefully backed the heavily loaded vehicle up to the edge of the rose garden and pulled the load release lever.

Irving and Carol have another hobby now. And it hasn't changed their lives much. Except for the elimination of roasted capon from their diets. Their oven is too full of chilled baby cobras.

Another one of our neighbors we call "The Expert." What he doesn't know just *hasn't* been printed in *Reader's Digest*. This mahatma lost me on the first day that we met when he suggested that I feed my dogs carrots. "Good for their teeth," he said. This may be true, but if you take a carrot and cut it up into stars, crescents, gingerbread men, and Kewpie dolls with a cookie cutter before feeding it to a dog, it will be eliminated from your dog in exactly the same form the next day. There is no way a dog's digestive apparatus can handle carrots except to get rid of them as rapidly as possible. I'm sure this dog expert would feed rabbits horsemeat and knuckle bones. "Good for their eyes, y'know."

For some strange reason The Expert likes us and is always dropping by to advise us on country living. Always as he leaves he yanks a few green stems from our garden—dismissing them as weeds that must be gotten rid of before they get out of hand. We have lost some of our most important and expensive plantings by this route.

After three years of depredation by this local nihilist, we have verged on panic at his approach. When we see him trudging up the drive toward our house, we quickly dash out the back door to our garden and start to careen around—madly covering up everything with long strands of curtains and draperies. When The Expert glances out the window and sees this untidy mess, we tell him we've just dyed our draperies and kitchen curtains and are drying them—in the sun. This perfect alibi is a little hard to maintain during the frequent Connecticut thunderstorms. We finally came up with a line for *this* situation. We explain carefully that the curtains and draperies needed streaking because we're doing the whole house over in the new psychedelic style.

The Expert, I'm sure, is influenced greatly by his homelife, where apparently his opinion about everything and anything means absolutely nothing. We always offer him a drink, but he always refuses —then he asks Reiko for a cup of coffee and adds, "Put a little brandy in it." This is the tip-off, as my psychiatrist friends say. That and the fact that he never brings his wife with him when he visits us and always refers to her, strangely enough, as "Godzilla." That is the tip-off even for us *laymen* who don't know anything about the meaning of "life" or *why* we're *happy*.

The Expert starts his monologues with a question like: "Did you know that Cleopatra was Jewish?" Or, "In ancient Mesopotamia they used chopsticks—the Chinese swiped the idea from them." Or, "A horny woman is usually very intelligent." These observations are very hard to dispute—unless you happen to be an Egyptologist, an ancient Mesopotamian, or an oversexed Rhodes scholar.

I never argue with The Expert; I simply increase

the dosage of brandy in each succeeding cup of coffee. Then, when he is ready to go home, I point him toward the Purdy Sloat Memorial Swamp, and ask *my* guardian angel to guide him.

chapter 3

OUR CHARMING NEXT-DOOR NEIGHBOR, whom we now call "The Thing," said to me one day after she moved in and was having trouble finding help, "I was *born* with servants and I am going to die with servants."

I advised her that if that was her plan, she'd better buy a used Time Machine from the Wells estate and set it for reverse.

When we first moved into this charming Outer Suburbia paradise, we inherited a maid from the previous owners. We kept her because "she knows where everything is"—like the *booze.*

This treasure from the world of Ajax and Brillo was by name "Gigi." Something warned me of trouble ahead when Gigi showed up the first day wearing harem trousers and a tiara. I thought it was one of the Supremes—on her way home from a Truman Capote party. I didn't know whether to bow or salaam—or throw myself at her feet and swear eternal fealty to the Land of Oz.

Stunned, I tendered in a small voice, "Gigi?"

"You *know* it!" she said. And slithered into the kitchen for a cup of coffee.

After an hour or so Reiko and I crouched in one corner of the living room and silently wondered when Gigi was going to start being our maid. Actually we never did find out.

Gigi was supposed, by some mysterious gentlemen's agreement, to show up for work at 9:00 A.M.—which she did for the first two days. She'd roar into the driveway in her white Cadillac convertible with its crinkly fenders and its rust trim. We had no agreement about using the back door, which led to the kitchen and a change room where she could change into something less comfortable, so Gigi would mince up to the front door and ring the ship's bell, which served as a warning that visitors were at the gates. This bell was another priceless treasure left behind when the previous owner fled. A few sessions with this bell could damage your auricular nerves permanently. And also make your nose bleed and cause cataracts. Gigi used this bell like it was wake-up time in cell block eleven. Every time she'd arrive, Reiko, Bobby, and I would flatten ourselves against the ceiling like a family of terror-struck lizards.

The 9:00 A.M. starting hour didn't last very long. After four days that was it. One day when she arrived just in time to fix lunch (for herself), I asked her where she had been and she said to the hospital. She had had her appendix out. I didn't mind that Gigi was blessed with the gift of imagination, but I felt that she was pressing, and when I suggested that one can't have one's appendix removed in the morning and report to work in the afternoon, she left. After finishing her lunch.

Gigi always showed up with more than a hint of beer on her breath. I didn't mind this too much because she could still steer a vacuum cleaner around and past any heavy accumulation of dirt without losing control on the fast corners. But during the second week of her forced labor with us, she arrived with a full load of the hard stuff. Every time she exhaled, the whole house was instantly sterilized by a monsoon of bourbon. Later, when I went into the kitchen to check up, I found her doing the limbo under the ironing board. Four hours later, I checked up again and she was still under the ironing board. When I called "Gigi!" she opened one eye and said, "Play it again, Sam."

Gigi's work, we wanted to think, was to keep the house clean, a task she approached with all the enthusiasm of a condemned felon on the twelfth and thirteenth step. A lighted cigarette permanently dangled from the side of her rubber lips. It has never been explained why she didn't explode in a ball of fire, while using all those cans of cleaning fluid labeled "Caution—Do not use near open flame!" Or why she didn't die a horrible death from a "Do Not Inhale" container or "If taken internally—do not induce vomiting!" can. This last has always puzzled me; on the surface I always felt that vomiting would be more or less involuntary after a slug of Drano. One day Gigi removed the cigarette from her mouth (leaving a little filter-tipped hole) and asked us if we needed someone to take care of the "grounds." Before we could answer, she told us confidentially that her husband was a landscape artist and just *happened* to have an hour open and would be able to fit us into his schedule if we acted quickly. We did, and seven minutes later we had a landscape artist mowing the lawn. Exactly eleven minutes after that the landscape artist came to the door and said that would be fifteen dollars. When I was silly enough to ask for what, he said for mowing the lawn, trimming around the trees, and spraying the elms. When I asked, "What about plowing the back forty and sowing the winter wheat?" he said, "Mr. Douglas, a man can only do so much in one day—fifteen dollars."

I said, "Now wait a minute, Buster!"

He said, "Claude."

I said, "Okay—Claude. Mr. Buttleman, who used to own this place, told me he only paid you ten dollars."

Claude rapidly became aghast. He blanched (as much as he could) then became hysterical. He said that his fee had always been fifteen dollars and if I didn't believe him I could come down and look at his books. When he said his "books," he made them sound as if they were closely guarded by Price, Waterhouse.

I gave Claude the fifteen dollars and my "blessing"

—and sure enough two weeks later he came down with leprosy.

Gigi isn't with us anymore either. She called one morning and said she was going to the hospital and having her appendix removed *that* morning. When I reminded her that she had had her appendix removed some three or four weeks before, she immediately agreed and said that she was actually calling from Columbia University and that she was going back to college. Knowing that she had been a drop-out from the sixth grade, I asked her what she was going to major in and she said maybe she wouldn't go to College, but would visit her sister in Miami Beach. That was the last we heard from Gigi—except a postcard from Miami Beach, where she wrote she had just had her appendix removed.

Many of our friends and neighbors have imported servants from South America. These South American imports have been well trained in their duties—one of which is answering the telephone. This alone has been a giant step toward avoiding any contact with the outside world. With a Brazilian, Venezuelan, Paraguayan, or Guatemalan maid, you are guaranteed the privacy of the tomb. If you are away and someone calls you and the maid answers, *you* will never know. And if you call someone with such a maid, *they* will never know. But—you will never *know* that you will never know, and the other party will never know that *you* will never know. It's a foolproof system.

But the lack of communication ends in your little domain. On the outside this girl, this shy creature from the mahogany forests of the Argentine or the inaccessible peaks of Peru, this awkward, inhibited, timorous violet, knows *everybody* in town. When she's not taking messages for you, she's on the phone talking to the whole world—babbling away in what sounds like Spanish Swahili with a dash of Bongo Bongo Bongo I don't wanna leave the Congo. She has ten thousand girl friends who apparently all come from the same mahogany forest or Peruvian peak which she comes from. On her day off, she shrugs away any proffered assistance and zooms into the big city like a hippie on her third time around.

Soon, of course, these Bambis of the Brazilian bush tire of kids, pots, pans, and slopping the suburban hogs. No matter what their agreement with the Latin-American Employment Agency, they're off to see the Wizard, and you have to break in a new Mato Grosso fawn.

Some families up here in Vigoro Birdland have English nannies—brought here protestingly to handle our little Colonial juvenile delinquents and to teach them the Queen's English. The families who have had the good fortune to charm one of these red-scrubbed-cheeked chimeras into their humble abodes never speak above a shaky whisper from that day forward. It is difficult to believe how Britannia could have possibly lost control of the waves with these formidable dreadnaughts still in active service.

Herb Cameron, who turned Anglophile for a short period in his disordered scheme of things, brought one of the first English nannies ever to be seen in Old New Litchridge. Herb, who has four children—all boys and all guaranteed to make the FBI's ten most wanted list with no trouble—thought an English nanny might be good for them.

Herb's boys immediately hated her because she didn't look like Greer Garson. Herb tried to explain that even Greer Garson doesn't look like Greer Garson anymore, but they would have none of it. Marvin, Herb's oldest son, said she looked like Winston Churchill. A couple of weeks later, Herb had to agree when he caught her smoking a cigar and drinking brandy. In bed. With Marvin.

This episode would have devastated a less unbiased father, but Herb Cameron has a special tolerance for the unexpected. He reasoned that any boy who has a thing for Winston Churchill would be less likely to start a Communist cell in the eighth grade.

chapter 4

THE OLD NEW LITCHRIDGE ADVERTISER editorially screams week after week: "Why don't the people who live in Old New Litchridge *shop* in Old New Litchridge????" The answer is they *do*. Once.

The shopkeepers of Old New Litchridge are a special breed. Every store is a hobby shop. Apparently run as a hobby. Something to keep the owner un-busy.

I have been feud prone with anyone in trade ever since I was shortchanged during my first visit to a house of ill repute, as they used to be called. After I had arrived home from this lovely experience, I discovered that the madam had not only shortchanged me, she had given me the fifteen cents in Canadian money. It was almost thirty-two years later, in Montreal, that I spent this money, and then I discovered that it was counterfeit. *This* madam was very nice about it. She told me not to worry—Canada really didn't expect to make any money out of Expo '67.

It didn't take me very long to get several hot feuds going nicely when we first moved up here to IBM-land. The first was with the Old New Litchridge Stationery and Gift Shoppe. I had bought a two-dollar glass vase (to keep pencils in) for eight dollars. I got it home before I discovered it was cracked. When I brought it back, the proprietor of the shoppe, whose face resembled a large mildewed eggplant, and whose breath, under pressure, could have been used to stamp out the Dutch elm disease forever, informed me that the base had not been cracked when it had left his place of business. When I explained to him that my hobby wasn't cracking vases and then returning them, he smiled—with the aid of two strings attached to the corners of his mouth—and said he was sorry, but he just couldn't think of exchanging a cracked vase, and would I mind, but it was Wednesday and all the stores in Old New Litchridge closed at noon. When I found myself on the street as he bolted the door and lowered the shades, I had the feeling that I was going to have to keep my pencils in an abandoned kangaroo pouch.

Luckily I had a charge account with this stationery store, so when the monthly bill came—as it did for nearly three years—I ignored it. Later I saw the very *same* cracked vase; it was on Herb Cameron's mantelpiece.

"Bought it at Ye Olde Antique Shoppe out on Route 7—only paid sixty-five dollars for it. Used to belong to Dolly Madison," said Herb. "She musta dropped it."

There are only eighteen stores in Old New Litchridge where the goods and services are excellent. One is the Old New Litchridge Bookstore. The other seventeen are liquor stores. The bookstore does not deliver, but the liquor stores have hundreds of little Volkswagen trucks on the road day and night. On Saturday night they're backed up for blocks waiting for the Main and Maple streetlight to change. The competition is fierce—among the customers, not the liquor stores.

One *hardware* store is run by a charming couple by the name of Mr. and Mrs. Harvey Brown. The first time I went in to pick up a box of sterilized thumbtacks and if possible a sterilized hammer. Mrs. Brown, whose given name was Gladys said, "Ask Harvey." When I asked Harvey, he said, "Ask Gladys." And that's the way it went every time I entered their hardware store. It was either "Ask Harvey" or "Ask Gladys," until one day they hired a local high-school dropout to assist. From that day on it was "Ask Fred." Fred wore a hearing aid from which he had craftily removed the batteries.

The other Old New Litchridge hardware store,

Millman's, did a fabulous business, but it was always on the verge of bankruptcy, because nobody ever paid his bills. This seemed to be one of the Fun City aspects of Old New Litchridge—the size of the bill you were able to run up at Millman's and the length of time you were able to avoid paying it gave you a certain prestige. A certain aura of celebrity. It only gave Mr. Millman gas. He was the largest single purchaser of Alka-Seltzer east of the Rockies. When Mr. Millman burped, most seismographs recorded it.

Mrs. Fink, which I'm not too sure isn't her name, runs the local kiddie shop, specializing in everything for the child from three to six. Mrs. Fink, who I feel must be plagued by something we don't know about —like Spanish crotch hives (Tabasco seasoned)— speaks, as the Pequot Indians used to say, with a forked tongue. She doesn't attract customers. Only opponents. When a mother and child—or children— enter her webbed shop, she flashes her Poli-gripped fangs in her best Bride of Frankenstein smile. This is the last of social amenities. From that moment on she loses her charm. If a mother asks the price of a pair of snow pants she snarls, "Do you want 'em or don'tcha?" If the mother is new in town and still *insists* upon knowing the price, Mrs. Fink picks up a sawed-off pool cue which she keeps for just such occasions.

For the past three years Mrs. Fink has been chosen as the Connecticut Mother-of-the-Year. By the Fairfield County Wolverine Breeders' Association.

The charming couple who are only charming to each other, and this is supposition) who run the toy store are also very annoyed when you come in to buy a toy. They both skulk behind a little counter at the front of the store and do not arise when a customer enters. If you say you just want to look around, they know right away you're a phony. Whoever heard of a parent who just wanted to "look around a toy store? The male half of this charming couple immediately jumps up and starts more than obviously adjusting the shoplifting mirrors, while his hippogriff mate keeps you covered with a laser gun. With this attitude, their inventory must change very little, if at all. I don't know what they do with all those toys. Maybe they *play* with them. I can't imagine them playing with *each other*. Still—with these new drugs—?

Firewood is something you must have ready access to if you live in Old New Litchridge and would like at least to have a fighting chance with the Cozy Oil Company (who, during a cold spell, has its big fat hose shoved into your oil hole every other day.

As an author who smokes a pipe and has his picture taken by Bruno of Hollywood for the dust jackets of his books once said: "Looking into the flames of an open fire brings back nostalgic memories and conjures up pleasant pictures of days gone by." An open fire may do this for him, but for me; all I get out of it is how much the goddamn firewood cost.

When called upon to explain the sudden escalation of firewood prices, Mr. Abruzzi, the firewood man, patiently—too patiently, I thought—explained that the price had gone up because of shipping charges. Living in an area where there is firewood for miles and miles in *any* direction, I asked him what the hell that meant. Shipping charges??? Mr. Abruzzi scratched his armpits (both at the same time), then massaged his crotch with a lot more enthusiasm, then asked me what was the question? I said, rather too loudly, "The shipping charges on *firewood*—where the hell does it come from?" "Oh," he said, "Hong Kong." I lost my poise completely and screamed, "Hong Kong! What the hell is the matter with *local* firewood?" He said, "Nothing—but everybody around here wants to charge everything on their Diners' Club card, and this is the only way we can do it."

I'd still rather have local firewood,—elm, hickory,

apple, or maybe oak. The aroma, if not exotic, is better. Hong Kong firewood smells like a Chinese laundry burning down with a load of Zero Mostel's wet ski clothes.

Plumbers have been discussed in many *other* classics, but may I add my small contribution to this one? Our plumber, Demetrius Moncton, and I have a *joint* checking account. This I did to keep him happy and to keep him coming. Demetrius Moncton is a very good plumber, and nothing is too much trouble for him to fix, so long as he can buy a few more shares of Standard of New Jersey or maybe a new mink trench coat for the little woman or *something* out of each little repair job. When we complained that our "guest" toilet sounded like the "Overture of 1812" every time it was flushed, Demetrius took it apart and showed us why. One of the intricate parts was marked: "Crane—1812."

It was a sad day when we lost Demetrius, but I guess it was the way he would have wanted to go. Somehow he got his foot caught in his Sewer-rooter, and the last we saw of him he seemed to be waving "bye-bye" in a ridiculously exaggerated circular motion as he gurgled downward and out of sight around the bend. Even though he is gone, we feel it was worth it. We haven't heard the "Overture of 1812" since. Just Brahms "Lullaby." As played by the Tijuana Brass.

John's Sports is the name of the local sporting goods emporium, which works out nicely. John's Sports seems to have somebody in the purchasing department who is queer for canoes. I say this because John's Sports is vastly and continuously and dangerously overstocked with canoes. If you so much as swing around suddenly while trying on Apache war bonnets, you are likely to start an *avalanche* of Indian boats.

Why John's Sports stocks canoes is a question for the gods, because no one has ever been known to buy one. Not in Old New Litchridge. If they want to go from one place to another by water, they buy a Mustang with pontoons.

I think John's Sports, outside of its obvious deficiency in stock balancing, has the most interesting salesman in town. He is wild. Disorganized. Cooperative and nearsighted. And he is the head of John's Sports gun department. This is like putting Buddy Hackett in charge of nuclear testing. His enthusiasm I think is what makes him stand out from the crowd. If you want to buy 12-gauge shotgun shells and he happens to be out of them, he shoves a box of 20-gauge shells at you. "Take them," he says. "If they don't fit, bring them back." They don't fit, but because of this nut's wild enthusiasm and insistence, I've tried.

The golden rule of "There's no such thing as an unloaded gun" is one rule this carefree potential assassin has never heard of. He points pistols, shotguns, and highpowered rifles, inadvertently, at anyone in the store and snaps the trigger. Of course everybody immediately hits the floor when he picks up a weapon, but so far, strange as it seems to the odds makers, there has been no unpremeditated massacre at John's Sports. But one day, I'm sure, some local practical joker will load a few of those Winchesters, Webleys, Remingtons, Colts, and Smith and Wessons, and it will be *Hallelujah, Baby* at the Stamford Shroud Boutique.

No book about this part of picturesque New England would be complete without some mention of the Connecticut Light and Power Company—a *profit* organization. It eases the pain of paying your electric bills in such a lovely way. I have in front of me now one of its little personal notes it always thoughtfully sends with all of its bills. I feel that the world should know about at least *one* large utility company that is *all heart*. This is what the note says:

JANUARY was the month that was cold! Very cold! Bitter cold! The coldest!
The seven-day cold wave that began January 7th actually set three new coldest day records: On January 8, 9, and 12.
In terms of degree days—a standard for measuring cold weather—this winter's heating system numbered 3,196 degree days as of January 17th.

Pretty goddamned long winter!

It was a record-breaking month for us, too! YOU demanded more CL & P service because the weather demanded it. YOUR heating system worked harder. So did YOUR hot-water heater, range, and other appliances. YOU also used more lights and watched more TV.

All this just to explain why our January electric bill was eighty-seven dollars. I don't care what anybody says—they're sweet.

Incidentally, we spent the whole month of January in Miami Beach.

chapter 5

OLD NEW LITCHRIDGE WAS SETTLED IN 1641 by a sharp old man with a dull lawn mower. The old man is long gone, but the lawn mower still operates (whenever a newcomer moves to town).

The land in Old New Litchridge, before the coming of the white pearl, was owned by the Pequot Indians—who were later massacred for their impudence. The land then passed into the hands of the Reverend Hiram Tankoos, who, being very friendly with King Charles II of England, obtained a Charter from His Majesty. This charter gave the Reverend Tankoos all the land from Long Island Sound to Seal Beach, Oregon, whose Indians were scheduled for massacre at a later date. In return, the Reverend Tankoos promised to bring gold to King Charles and God to Connecticut. Shortly after this, King Charles died—according to Suzie, the *Daily News* society columist, who *should* know, because she's always *right there* when the "in" things happen.

The Reverend Tankoos never found gold in Connecticut, but he *did* build churches—by the thousands. He would build eight or nine different churches in clusters, which he called "Piety Plazas." These churches he sold off to different denominations.

The Piety Plaza in Old New Litchridge is called "The Next Acre to Heaven," and whether God dwells in *each* one of them is a question asked each Sunday in every church about all the *other* churches in Old New Litchridge.

In the beginning, the Congregational Church was

the established church of the Colony of Connecticut, and in those days was the A & P of religion.

Later on, some groups broke away and became Methodists, Baptists, Latter-day Saints and Jews. Some even became Italian.

After we moved to Old New Litchridge, I asked the Old New Litchridge Historical Society for additional facts about the area.

One of the ancient documents the librarians unearthed for me was a 1644 copy of the minutes of a powwow with the Indians over the purchase of land. So far as I have been able to decipher it, the proceedings went something like this:

The meeting was called to order by Nathaniel Burcott, Proprietor, of Stammfoordt Towne, and Method Bradford, Proprietor, of Weestporte. Those present being the members of the Connecticut Colony Land Purchasing Company, Ltd., and the Chiefs of the Siwanogs, the Paugussetts, the Mohicans, and the Nipmucks. The pipe of peace was passed around and a feast of roast dog was enjoyed by all. After the acorn coffee and dandelion brandy, the discussions began:

NATHANIEL BURCOTT: I think we all know why we are all here.

CHIEF PONASS OF THE SIWANOGS: Yeah.

CHIEF POTATUCK OF THE MOHICANS: Why?

CHIEF PONASS: Shut up.

NATHANIEL BURCOTT: We would like to buy Indian lands.

CHIEF POTATUCK: Jesus Christ! More???

CHIEF PONASS: Shut up.

METHOD BRADFORD: We are willing to pay a fair price.

CHIEF POTATUCK: Ho! Ho! Ho!

NATHANIEL BURCOTT: What's wrong with three cents a square mile?

CHIEF PONASS: Four cents sounds better. Nice even number.

CHIEF POTATUCK: Which land you wanna buy?

NATHANIEL BURCOTT: All the land between the Six-Mile River, the Eight-Mile River and the ocean —then north as far as an Indian can paddle a canoe one day from sunrise to sunset.

CHIEF POTATUCK: That crap again.

METHOD BRADFORD: I beg your pardon, Chief?

CHIEF POTATUCK: I said "that crap again." The last time we had a land deal like that you guys picked the longest day of the year and you used three different Indians to do the paddling.

CHIEF PONASS: Yeah—Potatuck is right. You screwed us, just because all Indians look alike.

METHOD BRADFORD: *I* didn't say all Indians look alike.

CHIEF POTATUCK: But they *do*. I can't tell one god-damn Indian from another.

NATHANIEL BURCOTT: How about it?

CHIEF PONASS: How about what?

METHOD BRADFORD: How about the land we want to buy?

CHIEF PONASS: I dunno. How about a little brandy?

NATHANIEL BURCOTT: We're not supposed to give liquor to the Indians. We made that up when we first landed here on the *Mayflower*.

CHIEF PONASS: You think the Indians can't handle their liquor? Is that it?

METHOD BRADFORD: We're afraid you'll get high and start a war or a massacre or something.

CHIEF PONASS: We don't start massacres.

METHOD BRADFORD: How about that time in Deerfield?

CHIEF PONASS: Oh, yeah, Well—maybe once in a while. You know it's pretty goddamn boring being a peaceful Indian. We gotta have a little action.

NATHANIEL BURCOTT: Quite a bit of action at Deerfield from what I understand.

CHIEF POTATUCK: Well, the boys *did* get outa hand a little bit.

METHOD BRADFORD: Out of hand a *little bit!* The "boys" killed everybody in the village!

CHIEF PONASS: Time heals all wounds.

CHIEF POTATUCK: Hey, that's very good, Chief. Mind if I write that down?

CHIEF PONASS: Not at all, but gimme credit.

METHOD BRADFORD: We're getting sidetracked. What about the land?

CHIEF PONASS: What do you want to do with the land?

NATHANIEL BURCOTT: We want to clear it and plant crops.

CHIEF PONASS: Cut down the trees?

METHOD BRADFORD: It's the only way we can plant crops.

CHIEF PONASS: If you cut down trees, no more trees—and no more trees, no more animals to hunt or birds to catch and eat and no more fish.

NATHANIEL BURCOTT: No more *fish* if we cut down trees? Would you care to explain that, Chief?

CHIEF PONASS: No.

METHOD BRADFORD: Come on, it's getting late and this peace pipe just don't taste the same. Let's make a deal for the land or else.

CHIEF POTATUCK: Or else what? You'll bring the soldiers and take it away from us anyway.

NATHANIEL BURCOTT: Something like that.

CHIEF PONASS: Three cents a square mile?

METHOD BRADFORD: That's the price.

CHIEF POTATUCK: All the land between the Six-Mile River and the Eight-Mile River and as far north as an Indian can paddle a canoe in one day?

NATHANIEL BURCOTT: Yeah.

CHIEF PONASS: Waddya think, Potatuck?

CHIEF POTATUCK: I think it stinks, but waddya gonna do—these white bastards are organized and we Indians ain't.

NATHANIEL BURCOTT: Wait a minute, Chief. We white bastards don't like that kinda talk.

CHIEF PONASS: Sorry.

CHIEF POTATUCK: White bastards mighty sensitive all of a sudden.

METHOD BRADFORD: Now look, you two, if you're gonna get cute about this, we might just start a little investigation on you Indians. The questions might be embarrassing, like, "Where are you getting those French-made guns?"

CHIEF POTATUCK: There's a feller—Lucky Pierre—who—

CHIEF PONASS: Shut up, stupid! Look, white men, it's a deal. You can have the land, and gimme back my peace pipe. Where do I make my *X*?

NATHANIEL BURCOTT: Right here, Chief. You won't regret this.

CHIEF POTATUCK: Ho! Ho! Ho!

Mr. Nathaniel Burcott then made a motion for the meeting to be concluded and the motion was seconded by Mr. Method Bradford.

I found from a later document that this deal was not too profitable for the colonists, because the Indian who was supposed to paddle his canoe north ran into a rock just three feet from his starting point and drowned. The land between the two aforementioned rivers was twenty-six miles long, but only three feet wide. The Bradford-Burcott housing development really, according to the *History of the Colony of Connecticut*, never got off the ground.

Old New Litchridge is glutted with old houses which go back to Colonial times. Some of them are quite interesting; for instance, the Gatch-Snith-Comstock-Loder-Prissey house at the corner of Cobbleskill Road and Skunk Creek Drive. This was the house where George Washington was refused a room for the night. It seems that the house at that time was owned by the original owner, Miss Samantha Gatch, a spinster who thought that the Revolutionary War was immoral, and refused to have its commander in chief in her house. Washington had made a mental note not to appoint her as Ambassadress to Luxembourg when the war was over, and moved across the street to the Thorne-Fairweather-Ewing-Macrae-Evans-Esty-Findlay house, where he was welcomed with open arms and a hot toddy. Later, according to legend and/or fact, it was discovered that Miss Gatch's disapproval of the war was triggered by the peculiar circumstance of her having given refuge to a company of Hessian soldiers, whom she had sequestered in her attic, and who escaped to the British lines as soon as Miss Gatch's vigilance was relaxed. It seems that Miss Gatch was an Early American nymphomaniac, and although the Hessians were mercenaries, they didn't think they were getting paid *that* much.

The Penrose - Edes - Elkins - Gaylord - Bloodgood house which was located at Pansy's Mill and Midge Ridge roads had once been a roadhouse or inn, and had been run, when it first opened, by Blacknose the pirate. Blacknose was a relatively unknown pirate and preyed mostly on the shipping on Long Island Sound. He never picked up any booty from the Indies destined for Spain, but he collected quite a group of untidy early Colonial surfers and water skiers, which he sold at considerable profit to the Bridgeport Dog Food Company.

The Penrose - Edes - Elkins - Gaylord - Bloodgood house was probably the oldest house in Old New Litchridge. It was still equiped with Indian shutters which could be closed in case of an Indian raid or an Indian Peeping Tom. Or both. The old taproom is still intact, its exposed beams covered with two hundred years of soot. This is the room which the Bloodgoods, the present owners, use as their dining room and, having eaten there may I compliment the Bloodgoods here for having the *dustiest soup* in New England.

The P-E-E-G and Bloodgood house was built in the last quarter of the seventeenth century, and everytime the Bloodgoods lean too heavily on the wall, they find another fireplace. The wall then is immediately ripped out and the ancient fireplace faithfully restored. A few months ago the *last* wall in the Bloodgood house was ripped out, and the last Colonial fireplace was faithfully restored, and now the Bloodgoods have the only house in Old New Litchridge (or anywhere) with absolutely no place to hang a picture. The whole house is one vast assembly line of fireplaces. The original owner, Mr. Clyde Penrose, must have, according to Herb Cameron, belonged to the Fireplace-of-the-Month Club.

The "mud room" seems to be a carry-over from Colonial days, and the Penrose-Edes-Elkins-Gaylord-Bloodgood had a dandy—a large twenty-by-twenty-foot room, filled almost to capacity with mud. Why the Colonials saved mud no one has ever explained. Mrs. Bloodgood thinks it may have been because in the early days. A—1 mud might have been scarce, or maybe there was nothing else to save.

The taproom has a most unique conversation piece. During the Revolutionary War it seems that the inn had been surrounded by the British who fired almost fifty cannonballs at point-blank range. Construction being what it was in those days, they bounced right off the stout planking and timbers. But in the east wall of the taproom, there is embedded *one cannonball,* giving evidence that the colonist fired back. It also gave evidence of their courage, if not their brilliance. Shooting a cannon at the enemy from inside a windowless room was not the smartest thing the Minutemen ever did.

Every spring, or maybe it's fall, or then again it may be January first—I don't really know—the Old New Litchridge Garden and House Tour is held. Hundreds of nosy women pile into condemned buses and careen around town, inspecting Japanese beetle damage and roses named after patriots and/or tarts and what kind of furniture the big house on the hill has since the new neighbors have moved in. The furniture the new neighbors have is exactly what the old neighbors had because the new neighbors bought the old neighbors' furniture. This *is* disappointing!

Where these women come from or where they go *after* the tour is a mystery. They are never seen except on this day. Herb Cameron says the buses are owned by the Gloccamora Bus Company.

Benedict arnold was a local hero at the neighboring town of Ridgefield, when he and his courageous band of Colonials routed the British. There is a plaque on the hill where this skirmish took place, but the Ridgefieldians who erected this memento of Ridgefieldiana neglected to mention his leadership or even his participation, which I think is un-American. Just because later he sold a secret recipe for apple pandowdy to the British does not diminish his record up to that time. Herb Cameron attempted to paint "Benedict Arnold was here" on a number of stone walls in Ridgefield, but was promptly arrested because some of the older members of the Ridgefield American Legion thought he meant recently.

Poor Benedict Arnold—his biggest mistake was that he lived in an unenlightened age when betraying one's country was frowned upon. Even by college students.

We're in luck! The Old New Litchridge Historical Society has *just* published a lovely heavy volume about the old houses of Old New Litchridge! Here is an excerpt from the account of one of them:

> The Osborn - Rorshak - Halliday - Pabst - Finch-Pockriss-Mead house stands on the high hill overlooking Bushy Brook and Route 124. The house is a gray shingled saltbox with Moorish windows, and French Normandy portico carriage entrance and a fifty-foot Byzantine minaret, from which a splendid

view of the Old New Litchridge Country Club may not be seen.

The house was built in 1726 by one Trelawney Osborn, a farmer, blacksmith and shoe manufacturer who came to Old New Litchridge from the Colony of New Haven, with his bride, the former Miss Haverstraw Dormanchester, a very popular young lady to those who frequented the Old New Haven Grog Shoppe, where she had been an assistant barmaid.

Trelawney and Haverstraw had seventeen children, and gradually, year after year, had added to the main house until it now spread over three and one-half acres, until the fire, which occurred in 1743, which brought the house back to its original size rather suddenly.

Trelawney Osborn was killed in a head-on collision between two oxcarts on the Old Post Road and left his entire estate to the Danbury Institute of Selective Pornography—an organization which was striving to rid New England of its ingrained sense of propriety. Haverstraw Osborn, his widow, killed herself and her seventeen children by a prolonged period of German cooking. It took several years, but finally there were no more Osborns left.

The Danbury Institute sold the Osborn house to an Ernie Rorshak, for three pounds, fourteen shillings, and six pence. Mr. Rorshak, who had been a professor at Yale University, had been dismissed for teaching the theory that apes had descended from man. He had not only been dismissed, but had also been tarred and feathered. Some of the feathers were apparently unremovable, and Mr. Rorshak had to watch it in a stiff wind or he was likely to take off.

Ernie Rorshak married Deboray Doob, the daughter of an itinerant *wheelwright*. [I looked this up. A wheelwright is a man who, when anyone asks the question "Is that a wheel?" replies, "Right."] Deborah bore Ernie twenty-three children. *All albinos.* On a bright sunny winter's day when all the children were playing in the snow out in the backyard, Deborah noted in her diary, it was impossible to tell if there were any children there at all.

As time went by, Ernie Rorshak added much to the original house he had bought. To the original sun porch which ran clear across the front of the house, Ernie added another sun porch to keep the sun off the first sun porch. The legend from then on was that the Rorshaks had the coolest sun porch in all of New England. Ernie, being a Southerner at heart, served mint juleps on his new cool sun porch and enjoyed sitting and rocking with his family and friends and talking about the new sun porch, until one day tragedy struck! Ernie noticed that a teeny-tiny ray of sunlight was penetrating his now fabulous sun porch. Poor Ernie spent the next twelve years trying to find out where this tiny ray was coming from, but to no avail. He was rapidly becoming a broken man, when he couldn't solve this mystery, so in desperation he bought two three-foot maple trees and planted them in front of his sun porch.

This was in the year 1756, and today, 202 years later, those three-foot maple trees are now almost five feet tall.

In Connecticut you can't stint on fertilizer.

The Rorshak family finally passed into history. Poor Ernie died without ever knowing that the tiny ray of sunshine that presumably penetrated his sun porch was nothing more than a crack in his eyeglasses.

The house then passed from the Rorshaks to the Hallidays, the Pabsts, the Finches, the Pockrisses, to the present owners, Mr. and Mrs. Virgil Mead, who have done much to restore the house to its original state. They began by burning it to the ground.

Town meetings were the means used to govern

settlements such as Old New Litchridge. Again I am indebted to the Old New Litchridge Historical Society for the following excerpt from the minutes of a town meeting held on the twenty-eighth day of January, 1762:

1ST SELECTMAN OBADIAH HUMP: You good people of the village known as Stink Town are here tonight to change the name of the village to something more appropriate. Any suggestions?

2ND SELECTMAN JEB HUMP: How about "Stink City"?

1ST SELECTMAN OBADIAH HUMP: We're not big enough.

3RD SELECTMAN MURRAY HUMP: We *will* be! Or my name isn't Murray Hump!

1ST SELECTMAN OBADIAH HUMP: Everybody knows you're Murray Hump, so shut up! Give some of the other landowners and taxpayers a chance to suggest some idiot suggestions.

2ND SELECTMAN JEB HUMP: I like "Stink City."

1ST SELECTMAN OBADIAH HUMP: *You* like King George.

2ND SELECTMAN JEB HUMP: He kept us out of war, didn't he?

1ST SELECTMAN OBADIAH HUMP: Who cares about that?

MRS. CRISSY: *I* care about that! I don't want my boy to have to go off and fight in some foreign place like Danbury!

1ST SELECTMAN OBADIAH HUMP: All right! All right! Now let's have some order. We're here to pick a name for this village—a name that will stick—a name that we can be proud of. Any suggestions?

MR. KLINGFINGER: How about "Boston, Massachusetts."

2ND SELECTMAN JEB HUMP: Jesus H. Christ! Now there's a good suggestion!

MRS. REBECCA FRUNK: How about New "New Orleans"? Maybe somebody'll write a song about us, you know, like "'Way Down Yonder in New Orleans—with all them Dixie Queens—"

MR. JENSEN BOUTON: Speaking of queens, how are

we gonna get rid of that sonofabitchin' King George?

1ST SELECTMAN OBADIAH HUMP: Shhhhhh . . .That comes at another meeting, maybe forty years from now. Those things take time.

MR. JENSEN BOUTON: Well, I'm gettin' goddamn sick and tired of taxation without representation. Hey! I like that: "Taxation without representation!" How does that strike you, Jeb?

2ND SELECTMAN JEB HUMP: I still like Stink City.

MRS. SARAH GERALDTON: How about calling our village "Wilton"—after my cousin, Wilton Stamford?

MRS. CHARLES HARVEY: How about calling it "Stamford" after *my* cousin, Stamford Wilton?

1ST SELECTMAN OBADIAH HUMP: Look, ladies, we're not going to call this lovely community after *anybody's* cousin. Besides, there is a "Wilton" already.

2ND SELECTMAN JEB HUMP: Where?

1ST SELECTMAN OBADIAH HUMP: Over in Wilton—where the hell do you think?

MRS. SARAH GERALDTON: Then what about *New* Wilton?" or "*old* Wilton"?

MRS. CHARLES HARVEY: Or "Old Stamford"? Or "New Stamford"?

MRS. REBECCA FRUNK: Or "New Faces"?

1ST SELECTMAN OBADIAH HUMP: You know what I think ladies—I think we stopped burning witches a little too soon in New England.

MRS. REBECCA FRUNK: I've never been so insulted in my whole life!

1ST SELECTMAN OBADIAH HUMP: Then you're leaving?

MRS. REBECCA FRUNK: Don't be silly; I came here for coffee and cake and I'm going to stay until I get it.

2ND SELECTMAN JEB HUMP: "Stink City"—it has a ring to it.

1ST SELECTMAN OBADIAH HUMP: For Crissakes, Jeb, nobody likes that name but you.

MR. ORVILLE MURDLER: I like it.

1ST SELECTMAN OBADIAH HUMP: Mr. Murdler! What the hell are you doing here? Aren't you at the county poor farm?

MR. ORVILLE MURDLER: Yeah, I come down for some coffee and cake. The food at the poor farm is lousy.

1ST SELECTMAN OBADIAH HUMP: Well, you're not a taxpayer, so shut up. Now—any more suggestions?

3RD SELECTMAN MURRAY HUMP: I think I got it! Why don't we call it "*Litch Ridge*"?

MR. ORVILLE MURDLER: What the hell kind of name is that? What's a "litch"?

3RD SELECTMAN MURRAY HUMP: Shut up! You're not a taxpayer!

MR. ORVILLE MURDLER: I'd *still* like to *know*. What the hell's a "litch"?

MRS. REBECCA FRUNK: It must be something; they got a Litch*field*.

MR. ORVILLE MURDLER: Maybe *they* don't know either.

2ND SELECTMAN JEB HUMP: Wait a minute! They already got a Litchridge—on Route 4.

3RD SELECTMAN MURRAY HUMP: Then why don't we call it "New Litchridge"?

MRS. REBECCA FRUNK: They got that, too; it's the next town up from Litchridge.

3RD SELECTMAN MURRAY HUMP: That's no problem; we'll just call our town "*Old* New Litchridge." After all, *we* settled *here* before *they* settled up *there*. They still got Indians up there.

MRS. REBECCA FRUNK: We still got Indians *here!*

3RD SELECTMAN MURRAY HUMP: Sure, but we took care of that. We told them they were *Japanese*. They won't give us any trouble anymore.

1ST SELECTMAN OBADIAH HUMP: Then it's all decided, huh? We change the name from "Stink Town" to "Old New Litchridge." All those in favor of the name change signify by saying, "Aye." All those against, "Nay."

MR. ORVILLE MURDLER: Wait a minute! There's something I think you all should know.

3RD SELECTMAN MURRAY HUMP: What now???

MR. ORVILLE MURDLER: Well, I just looked out the window and as much as I hate to be the bearer of bad news . . . them Japs just scalped Old Lady Peltzer and now they're burning down the Stink Town Hotel!

1ST SELECTMAN OBADIAH HUMP: That's the *Old New Litchridge* Hotel!!!

chapter 6

THIS CHAPTER IS WRITTEN MORE OR LESS as a warning to city folks who intend to visit with their friends in Outer Suburbia. Unless you have practiced on a few expeditions to the Antarctic, the Gobi Desert, or the jungles of the South American rain forest—forget it. You're not ready. I speak not of hardship or creature discomforts—I am merely trying to prepare you for the wild panic that will seize you when you suddenly realize that you have journeyed into a vast and geographically unknown area, where compasses, maps, and other navigational equipment are useless. You will become hopelessly lost. Perhaps permanently. At some time during your frenzied search for a house number, a name on a mailbox, a street sign, there will be a sudden, horrendous tropical thunderstorm. The wind will reach hurricane strength. Trees will crash down across the road in front of you. Or it will start to snow. Lightly at first, then swiftly becoming a blizzard. Drifts five feet high block your path. It's the worst snow-storm since 1802. Then you see a signpost! "Route 33!" Quickly, by the flicker of a cigarette lighter you reread *all* of the soggy direction sheet so carefully prepared by Gus and Carol:

WHEN YOU REACH ROUTE 33 MAKE A LEFT -- IN THE DIRECTION OF RIDGEFIELD. YOU WILL TRAVEL APPROXIMATELY 1.5 MILES TO WILTON WOODS ROAD. MAKE A RIGHT AT WILTON WOODS ROAD. WILTON WOODS ROAD IS A HORSESHOE THAT COMES OUT ON ROUTE 33.

THERE ARE TWO RIGHTS OFF WILTON WOODS ROAD -- THE FIRST IS SNOWBERRY LANE, THE SECOND IS LONGMEADOWS LANE. MAKE A RIGHT AT LONGMEADOWS LANE -- OUR MAILBOX IS ON THE RIGHT. TURN LEFT AT OUR MAILBOX. YOU WILL PASS TWO HOUSES ON YOUR RIGHT AND THEN COME TO OUR MAILBOX. THE ROAD, AT THIS POINT, STARTS TO ELEVATE.

This may be it! You make a left. In the direction of Ridgefield. You travel approximately 1.5 miles—but there's *no* Wilton Woods Road. You travel approximately 1.6 miles—again there is no Wilton Woods Road. You try 1.7, 1.8, and 1.9, but—no Wilton Woods Road. You backtrack and try 1.4, 1.3, and 1.2 miles—*nothing.*

Your wife asks, "Why don't we stop and ask somebody?" You kill her. You haven't seen a light or a house or a filling station for three hours. You press the button to lower the car window because you think you've seen a mailbox. There's no name on it—just a four-letter word.

"Why don't we visit *them?*" suggestes your brother-in-law. You kill *him.* You press the button again; the car window does not respond. It hides down inside the relatively cozy warmth of the door. Snow starts drifting in through the window. The children want to build a snowman. You kill *them.*

Morning comes. You're stranded without gas somewhere. You don't know where. Someone is walking along the road. He stops. It's Gus.

"You're early," he says. "Dinner isn't till eight o'clock."

You kill Gus.

The above is, of course, an exaggeration, with one exception. Somebody *did* kill Gus.

Herb Cameron has approached the problem of guiding friends to his hearth in an extremely logical and methodical manner. A strange departure for him. Herb sends out a series of graduated maps long before the impending visit. The first is a map of the Western Hemisphere, followed in the ensuing days by maps of the United States, then the New England States, then Connecticut—then Fairfield County. Herb feels now that the prospective visitor is properly oriented, so he sends him the first map of Old New Litchridge itself—a map that was executed in 1649 by a William Trudge. This map is extremely decorative. The actual map itself is very small, but the edges all around it are brilliant with pictures of bears, deer, Indians, wild turkeys and fat-faced cherubs apparently blowing up a storm.

The map itself isn't much help today. It pictures only one thoroughfare—the old Danbury-Kansas City Post Road. Which follows an old Indian trail all the way. To date, no one has bothered to explain why there was so much Indian traffic between Danbury and Kansas City. Personally I would like to know. Wouldn't you, Crazy Horse?

Herb's next map of Old New Litchridge includes a few more roads, and included in the border decoration along with the bears, deer, Indians, and wild turkeys are a few tax collectors—in place of the windy cherubs.

This map was cartographed by the famous cartographer Zachary Coggeshall in 1775. Mr. Coggeshall, by nature Machiavellian, made two versions of this map, which he sold to both sides during the Revolutionary War. The confusion that resulted from this mad mad mad mad duplicity was unbelievable. For example, the Westport Country Playhouse was designated as a British fort on one version of Mr. Coggeshall's map, and marked as George Washington's headquarters on another, with the result that during the entire Revolutionary War the Westport Country Playhouse was under constant shellfire from both sides, which made it extremely difficult to try out new plays there in those days. The actors could hardly hear the audience.

The last map which Herb sends is a present-day map. Most of the decorative edges are gone. Only the tax collectors are left. Disguised as fat-faced cherubs. The route to Herb's house is traced out quite plainly in red ink, and no one experiences any difficulty until he reaches Route 33, which is on the northern edge of the map. Then you have to rely on a page of printed directions:

WHEN YOU REACH ROUTE 33 MAKE A LEFT-- IN THE DIRECTION OF RIDGEFIELD. YOU WILL TRAVEL APPROXIMATELY 1.5 MILES TO WILTON WOODS ROAD.

When Herb bought this place from Gus . . .

chapter 7

WE SEEM TO COLLECT ANIMALS, BESIDES two Doberman pinschers, which we acquired when we first moved to Old New Litchridge—a couple of years ago we bought a malamute. For those of you who are not Eskimo or Aleut, this word may throw you. A malamute is a dog, whom the moment little children see it they scream, "Oh, Mommie, look—a husky!" or "Papa—is that an Eskimo dog?" In order not to make Papa look like a dope, I wink surreptitiously at Papa and nod my head. Sometimes Papa thinks I'm a sneaky queer and quickly hustles his kid from my obnoxious presence. And sometimes Papa is a sneaky queer and *I* have to use one of the secret emergency exits at the A & P.

The malamute is not a husky or an Eskimo dog. According to the American Kennel Club, an organization devoted to pure breeding (aren't we all?), the malamute is a distinct and separate breed. We got Chibi (a Japanese name meaning cute) from the Chinook Kennels in New Hampshire. This is the same kennel that supplied the malamutes used as sled dogs for several of the Byrd Antarctic expeditions.

We picked him up at about seven o'clock in the morning one extremely cold, snowy January day. As we approached the pen where Chibi was, with Mrs. Seeley, the owner of the kennels, all fifty or sixty of the other penned malamutes started howling. With their heads thrown back and their necks extended, they howled and howled and howled. It was the most wonderful sound I have ever heard. Standing there in the deep New Hampshire forest, the snow-laden pines, hemlocks, and birches as a backdrop with long fingers of sunlight reaching between them, the world was all purple and gold and filled with the music of the wilderness. It was like the beginning of time.

That was the last time that Chibi ever howled. When we got him back to the pseudo-civilization of Connecticut, he seemed to have been struck dumb. We were crushed. We knew that we couldn't capture that magic moment in the wilds of New Hampshire, because one malamute can't sound like fifty, but a malamute who won't even try is like having a kid who doesn't get into fights on the school bus. Or taking LSD and never *going* anywhere.

We communicated with Mrs. Seeley and shé said "Don't worry, in time he will howl." But he never did. To him the full moon was just something that shone in his eyes when he was trying to get a little rest from us trying to get him to howl.

At first we tried to find a recording of howling malamutes which we could play to jog his memories of Old New Hampshire, or give him an idea of what was expected of $300 malamute. Try as we did, we could not find one single solitary recording of malamutes howling. This I could not understand. Whatever happened to the law of supply and demand?

Folkways Records was my last chance. This company has recordings of everything: lions, tigers, hippos, elephants, hyenas, alligators, beavers, moles, crickets, lizards, and so on and on and on. We bought them all, but although Chibi listened most attentively, he uttered not a sound. We thought we had him there for a moment when we played the gurgle of a python's digestive tract after eating three live pigs in a row. Chibi picked up his ears and cocked his head in his best "His Master's Voice" pose, but that's as far as it went.

Then, in final desperation, I had a wild thought. I bought every record that Sonny and Cher ever made, then waited for a night when the moon was very full, when I played them *all* at the *same time* on over a hundred borrowed record players. This didn't bring on any howls, but three units of the National Guard were here in twenty minutes. They thought it was Newark all over again.

When they saw that we only had a six-year-old *black* and *white* TV set, they knew right away that we couldn't be looters, and they doubted if we were Americans.

After this we gave up on Chibi. We loved him and if he didn't love us enough to howl it was okay with us. Then one day I read a book called *A Wolf in the Family,* by Jerome Hellmuth, an educator, author, animal lover who had taken a one-day-old wolf and raised it in the bosom of his family. Mr. Hellmuth's book is a warm, wonderful account of life with a wolf. Here, I thought, might be the answer to our howling problem—if Chibi could live around a howling wolf he might catch on, and I had always been attracted to this most misunderstood animal, who has been shot and poisoned out of most of the United States by sheer malice, stupidity and ignorance. So little is apparently known by the general public about the wolf, it astounds me, because so much has been written about this quite noble beast. And all of it most favorable. But enough for the defense. *Where* do you find a place that *sells wolves?* There aren't many. Not in the Yellow Pages, anyway. At first I wrote to a professional hunter, who advertises in *Alaska Sportsman* magazine. He advertised wolf hunts, but when I asked him to bring me back a live pup he declined, and I really don't blame him. Gunning down a defenseless animal is a helluva lot safer than bringing back a live one.

A few months went by and suddenly one day in a new issue of *Northern Dog News,* a small magazine concerning this subject, there appeared an article by a Miss Sandra Harris about her pet wolves. In no time at all we were corresponding furiously and she also sent me pictures of some of her animals. I needed no more. I couldn't *wait* until I had one, but I *had* to until they were born, which is in the spring. Six weeks later Tanuki, as we call him, arrived by United Air Freight from California. He weighed ten pounds and looked so small and forlorn in the little cage he arrived in. Today he is a year and a half old and weighs 150 pounds. And he *howls*—at *everything!* Jet planes whining overhead. Automobile horns. Ducks quacking in the brook. The moon. He howls when he is sad. He howls when he is glad. He howls when he is hungry and he howls when he is full. He is a great great howler. Far exceeding our dearest wishes and expectations. And Chibi, finally getting the message, howls right along with him.

It's heaven!

Old New Litchridge has no ordinances against howling wolves. You can only get a ticket if you have a rooster that crows. I know, because I spent half a day at the town hall looking through all the ordinances that have been passed since 1741. There is, now that I think back, an ordinance against having a rooster that howls or a wolf that crows. This ordinance was passed in 1768 when the 1st, 2nd and 3rd Selectmen were drunks. Also in those days they had a 4th Selectman who was an alternate drunk.

But getting back to my wolf, or I should say our wolf, because he loves Bobby and Reiko as much as he does me. Bobby slaps him all around and he takes it without ever retaliating except for a few playful growls. He outweighs Bobby by almost a hundred pounds, and if he wanted to he could tear him apart in five minutes and leave him in a mighty untidy little pile.

With me he plays differently. He crouches down behind a tree and springs on me unexpectedly (he thinks) and takes great pleasure in ripping jackets and shirts. Also he is an expert pickpocket. Almost invariably, unless I remember to guard against it, he gets the handkerchief out of my back pocket and then tears off into a corner and rips it to shreds. I've lost so many handkerchiefs they're working overtime in Manila.

When he was very small and didn't trust anyone, including me, he did bite me quite a few times with his tiny, knifelike baby teeth. I was afraid the doctor might not understand if I told him I had been bitten by a wolf in my backyard, so I simply said I had caught my hand on a nail. After about the fourth or fifth trip for medical aid, the doctor said, "Jack, I have an idea." "Anything at all, Doctor," I said, "anything at all." Then he said, "Why the hell don't you pound in that nail—or get rid of that wolf?"

For some reason, Tanuki didn't bite me anymore after this. For which I'm deeply grateful, because when I drove him to the vet's in Ridgefield, he always would lie down with his head in my lap all the way, and try to sleep. I kept thinking during these journeys—suppose he should have a nightmare and suddenly close those already massive jaws on my crotch? How would I explain this to my *ex*-loved ones? Or *anybody*?

Lately, when our screaming neighbor, Mrs. Kloompt, has been away on one of her pilgrimages to U. S. Steel—or wherever she goes to have her throat re-plated, Tanuki has been quite calm. After a few days of blessed silence he relaxes and accepts other strange noises and smells—and even people, although he does not cosy up to anyone except Reiko and Bobby and me. About as close as he can force himself to get is maybe a sniff, or a lick, or, if he likes the intruder, a small, friendly nip. This is the wolf's method of showing affection.

Some of our visitors to the wolf pen don't quite understand this. They react by immediately draining the blood supply from their faces, then hastily start examining their entire bodies for signs of the wound. Of course there isn't any, and when we try to explain that Tanuki never breaks the skin when he gives a love nip, this throws them into panic. Now they know they're bleeding great rivers—internally. I encourage this thought. I don't need any nervous friends. I have my own traumas to trample.

A wolf may seem like a strange pet for Suburbia, but last year when I wrote Dorothy Averback, a friend of ours in Beverly Hills, that we had one, she wrote back that she wasn't surprised at all that I had a wolf. What amazed her, she said, was that I hadn't bought a mountain lion.

Last week, by United Air Freight, from California in a little cage——————*

*Read all about it in: *The Neighbors Are Scaring My Mountain Lion.*

chapter 8

THIS MORNING, AFTER TIPPYTOEING OVER the empty beer cans, which are a permanent part of the Connecticut roadside decor, I reached our mailbox.

The mail as usual was fascinating. Caldors was having a sale. Sears was having a sale. The A & P was having a sale, and Standard & Poor's was most anxious to advise me on my stock portfolio. They were most anxious once before, and I bought their advice for $19.38. Immediately after cashing my check they gave me their first advice—for $800 more they would *really* tell me what to do with my portfolio. They seemed so earnest and sincere about the whole thing, I felt like a cad when I told them that I was getting the same advice *they* were *selling* from Merrill Lynch, Pierce, Fenner & Smith, Inc. for *nothing!* This aroused something in them and they turned on me like a wounded social worker. I have a feeling I haven't heard the last of *them*—mainly because *they* haven't heard the last of *me.* However—back to the real world where real things count—like the Old New Litchridge Bird Watchers Club. *They* know what life is all about. It seemed from the postcard they'd sent they wanted me to be on the lookout for saw whet owls, pine siskins, and California condors.

The card explained that if I saw any of the above I should call the Old New Litchridge Bird Watchers Club at 666-6666, which was their special emergency number.

They sounded more earnest and sincere than Standard & Poor's, so I rushed right down to John's Sports and bought a pair of high-powered German binoculars. I also bought a pair of gloves that were supposed to keep your hands warm as toast at subzero temperatures. This is an annual purchase. I don't know what kind of gloves the Eskimos wear, but if they ever tried *these* gloves, there wouldn't be an Eskimo from Greenland to Nome who could point.

The clerk at John's Sports sniggered as he added and padded the bill.

"What's so funny?" I asked.

"Nothing," he said. "I just didn't know you were a bird watcher."

"I'm not," I said, "I'm a U-boat commander." As a brilliant afterthought I added, "Heil Hitler!"

The clerk immediately snapped to attention, clicked his heels, and, with an upshot arm, echoed me. "I'm a veteran," he explained.

After I got my gloves and binoculars home, I sat at the living-room window (I wore my new gloves) because we were going through a period of fuel oil economizing. The gloves didn't keep my hands warm, but I felt they might ward off the Connecticut jungle rot. The binoculars worked fine. During the first hour of bird watching, I saw 4,216 sparrows, but no saw whet owls. No pine siskins. And no California condors. I was about to call up John's Sports and ask the clerk if he would exchange the binoculars for an Arnold Palmer opium pipe, when suddenly *there* they were: a saw whet owl, a pine siskin, and a California condor. All sitting on the same branch of the big old elm tree, which we had bought the year before when the next village was cutting down the forest to make way for a slum. The tree was lovely. At least a hundred years old and we bought it for $11.60—plus $700 cartage. But this chapter isn't about trees. As soon as I spied the saw whet owl, the pine siskin, and the California condor, I immediately knew the weakness in the Old New Litchridge Bird Watchers Club system: we hadn't been informed that these three would be traveling *together*. Like a French movie.

On the telephone Mrs. Gruns, president of the Old New Litchridge Bird Watchers Club, didn't seem too impressed that I had seen these birds. In fact she got quite nasty, in a Radcliffe manner, and informed me that California condors are confined to California, and because of "sportsmen" there were only about six or seven left in the world. When I protested that, according to my Quick Bird Identification Chart it *was* a California condor, she inferred by the innuendo chart that I was drunk. She said, "You are *drunk*." A*That's innuendo at Radcliffe.*) I took umbrage at this, because although I had had a few Martinis I was far from drunk. Not too far, I'll admit. Then quickly, I remembered that the postcard I had received from Mrs. Gruns' organization had specifically noted that we were to report any California condors. I asked her about that. I said, "How about that?" And she said, "Yes ... how about that? We are not only checking on *birds* in the Old New Litchridge district, but also at the same time—at the suggestion of Mr. Gallup—taking a poll of *drunks* in the same area!"

I felt this was pretty sneaky and said so. Mrs. Gruns was ready for me. She said, "Would you like it better if someone came to your door and said, 'I'm from the Gallup Poll—are you a drunk?' Or, 'Avon calling—are you a drunk?' "

I said I didn't think Mr. Gallup would ask such a question. Mrs. Gruns gave me a merry ha-ha. And asked if I had forgotten Kinsey. I hadn't, because I just happened to be in chapters nine, ten, and eleven—and I wish now that I had allowed my name to be mentioned.

There is great difficulty in watching birds in Old New Litchridge because of old prejudices. Anyone seen skulking through the woods carrying a pair of high-powered binoculars is immediately classified as a Peeping Tom. And nine and a half times out of ten that is right. Peeping Toms must be very frustrated in their chosen avocation because, in all my years in this lovely semi-New England community, I have never seen *any* woman whom I would like to see undress. Not at the A & P anyway. There may be some lovely women hidden somewhere back in the bush of some of the large estates, but they are apparently not allowed to visit the A & P unless they are heavily veiled. And guarded by eunuchs. Who are in turn watched over by Mary Poppins.

There is one man in our neighborhood who does his bird watching from the back of a horse. He is apparently a very wealthy man, because he has three butlers running ahead of him, releasing birds for him to watch. Once, when one butler's supply of birds ran out, this wealthy old gentleman got very angry, and for the rest of the bird-watching season the butler was forced to sit in an eagle's nest until the baby eagles hatched. Now when this poor man is asked why he doesn't sit down at the dinner table, he is hard pressed for an answer. Personally I think he should confess. It's not exactly like having a scar from Old Heidelberg but it should keep the conversation up to a high level.

I am not a bird watcher myself. I'm a rat watcher. The bread I throw out on the patio for the raccoons has attracted a whole Levittown of rats. They're wood rats so they really don't know too much about the bubonic plague but I hope to educate them gradually, and then when the time comes I would like to trap them (in Hava-Hart Humane Traps, of course) and release them at choice locations around town. Then I'll move in and buy whatever property my rats and I have made available from the survivors at a good price. It may not be ethical, but as one real-estate dealer said not long ago at a Kiwanis luncheon, "The bubonic plague is better than a firm offer."

I like rats but we may have overdone the whole project, because, although, according to U.S. Bureau of Sport Fisheries and Wildlife, wood rats do *not* come into your house, we have heard strange noises in the walls of our living room. These strange noises *could* be, our neighbors have advised us, the Wilstach ghost. The Wilstach ghost, it seems, is the restless spirit of a wealthy Old New Litchridge compost dealer, who was murdered in this very house by his wife. One morning for breakfast she fed him un-puffed rice and then puffed it. This ingenious lady was subsequently tried, found guilty, and released with a warning. She was pretty mad about the whole thing because the Court didn't give Green Stamps. At last report, Mrs. Wilstach is now living in Kansas City under an assumed name and working as a topless plumber.

Birds and bird watching have apparently always been important to Old New Litchridge. Once a month the Old New Litchridge Bird Watchers Club meets to hear a guest speaker. These are usually pretty dull affairs, unless of course you don't count the night they had Professor Pertwee of Princeton.

Professor Pertwee had, through the years, acquired a smattering of a reputation as a wit and a raconteur. His wit, as interpreted by the bird-watching fraternity, was quite daring. How daring Old New Litchridge was to find out. One wintry night last January, Professor Pertwee had finished his prepared address on the breeding habits of ostriches and penguins, and had launched with some enthusiasm into the question-and-answer period. Things went smoothly enough until Mrs. Hildebrand, the owner of Hildebrand Hill, and one of Old New Litchridge's first families, started asking questions: "What is the difference between a MacGillivray's warbler and Bachman's warbler? What color are the Bell's vireo's eggs? Why is a pileated woodpecker seen so seldom? Does the Carolina chickadee actually come from Carolina? Which is the best time of year to look for the common snow bunting? In the fall or in the spring?"

Professor Pertwee fielded these questions with the agility of an old bird-watcher lecture pro. Then his collar started to choke him and the muscles in his jaws tightened. He had had enough.

"Thank you very much, Madame," he said, without moving his lips. "Your questions have proved most illuminating."

"I have one more," Mrs. Hildebrand said, with a trace of challenge coloring her tone.

"But, of course," said the professor.

"What is a titmouse?"

"A titmouse, my dear lady," said Professor Pertwee, narrowing his eyes, as he stared at Mrs. Hildebrand, "a titmouse is a mouse with tits."

"Thank God," said Mrs. Hildebrand. "At last, someone has had the courage to tell us the truth."

"Amen," said the Old New Litchridge Bird Watchers Club.

chapter 9

THE OLD NEW LITCHRIDGE HORSEY SET IS not really much of a problem, but its members do take some getting used to. When Old New Litchridge had more open country than it has now, this group used to canter, trot, gallop, and jump wherever it pleased, and it still does—even if this involves tallyhoing across somebody's new pansy bed, or jumping a clothesline instead of an old rail fence. There is a story that goes the rounds regularly that Herb Cameron once rode his faithful old mare, Trixie-Baby, through twenty-seven living rooms of a new housing development which was unfortunately laid out exactly in the middle of one of Herb's favorite old bridle paths. This story is not true. It was twenty-seven *bed*rooms. This was at six o'clock one frosty fall morning, and there's been a sex blackout in that part of town ever since. Nervous young newlywedded housewives had been led to expect the voices of an angelic chorus—not the horrific sound of a horse snorting from both ends.

I am quite conversant with this side of the Old New Litchridge sporting set. Many a morning horses are ridden up to the big window of my ground-floor ivory tower, where I am startled from my daily chore of wooing the muse. Or, as Reiko put it once, "What's that mean—screwing a moose?" I am perfectly willing anytime to knock off work and chat, but our lawn doesn't take too kindly to feet—let alone hooves. The horses seem to be able to control themselves admirably until they reach our place. Then it's bombs away! I've tried following them around with my Little Miss Muffet Manure Spreader, but they kick me. The *riders*—

not the horses. The Horsey Set is so sensitive. Its members think that this equine ordure has some sacred significance. I don't know why. I've never heard of *any* race, no matter how primitive, that *ever* worshiped horseshit. Mouse turds, yes—but only by Pygmies. Anything any bigger *scared* them.

Most of the Horsey Set belongs to the Old New Litchridge Hunt Club, a venerable (according to its members) organization devoted to the pursuit of the fox. This is a very conservative hunt club, mainly because they only have *one* fox to pursue. And he is getting on in years. Half the time, during the hunt, they have to transport him across hill and dale in a golf cart—just letting him out every once in a while to give the hounds something to sniff and yelp at. Some of the hounds also have almost had it. They have their own special golf cart, with an open bottom so they can sniff without getting out. Also, for the older dogs: they are so asthmatic, there is a recording of hounds yelping, which the fox keeper plays at irregular intervals.

The horses used by the Old New Litchridge Hunt Club, from what I've seen from a distance, are rejects from Anheuser-Busch. They all wear blinders so they won't scare each other.

Huntsmen and women start the hunt at 6:30 A.M. with a hunt breakfast, which consists of huge quantities of any alcoholic liquid that mixes well, but not too well, with food, in lesser amounts. At noon (more or less and usually more) the gamekeeper blows his horn. This wakes him up. The hunters are summoned by an announcement over the loudspeaker in the bar. "Gentlemen, start your engines!" The hunters then gather in front of the clubhouse and proceed up the ramps to their respective saddles. Once strapped on, the hunt master blows his horn and releases the fox. Then he blows his horn again to wake up the fox. The fox, galvanized into a lethargic trot, heads for the nearest pasture, which takes quite some time because of the many stoplights en route. Finally he reaches open country—and the hunt is more or less on.

Some of the hunters never leave the hunt club grounds. Some give up after the third stoplight. The ones who reach the first pasture are usually sorry that they did, because by this time the hunt breakfast has begun to wear off and the fox is nowhere in sight. Or sometimes the fox is in sight but the dogs are not. The fox apparently uses Arrid because the dogs have a helluva time following him by scent alone. He usually has to stop every once in a while and *wave* to them. They wave back—wondering who the hell *that* is.

Some hunt days the fox doesn't feel up to it and the chief huntsman has to arrange to have a dead chicken dragged over the hunt course. This, of course, means that the *fox*hounds, who strangely enough seem to know the difference, have to be replaced with *dead-chicken* hounds. Sometimes a chicken isn't available and they have had to drag a dead club member. This practice, though, has been stopped. Too many people complained of the dust.

Some of the Horsey Set neither belong to the hunt club nor own a horse—they just like to get dressed up in jodhpurs and billow-assed pants and stride around slapping their thighs black and blue with their riding crops. Some of which are weighted. For masochists. Some, of course, are sadists and strike each *other* with their riding crops, the striker yelling "Tallyho!" and the strikee, "Yoicks!" Actually, these phrases are interchangeable. When you are a sadist it isn't the gift—it's the thought.

Those in the Doggie Set wear tweed underwear and smell from saddle soap—which they used on their tweed underwear. It has *cold power!*

Quite a few of the Doggie Set "show" their dogs at

dog shows. I go to all of them. Not for the dogs, but the people. I love to watch those enormous women with flaps on their shoes thundering around the show ring, alternately dangling and dragging a three-pound Chihuahua on a tiny chain. Then they stop and spread the dog's legs backward and forward—then they spread them a little farther. The judge, who looks as if he has Argyle blood, bends down and checks the animal for a pedigreed hernia.

The judges at a dog show are more enigmatic and inscrutable than any inscrutable Oriental could ever be. And they never let *me* know who has won. They go from dog to dog around the show ring, then suddenly the crowd breaks into wild applause. *They* know who has won, but *I* don't. It's like the ballet. I can't tell when I've seen a great *pas de deux* until the audience suddenly starts foaming at the mouth and beating each other with their wristwatches and screaming "Bravo, Rudy" or "Bravo, Margot" or "Bravo, Herbie" or whoever it happens to be.

This is the way it is at the dog show. Suddenly the lights go out, the show is over, and I don't know who has won. Actually, it doesn't really matter who wins at dog shows. Even the losers must get blue ribbons. I have never visited the home of a show dog owner who didn't have the walls of his cozy disinfectant-redolent den plastered from ceiling to floor with them. Maybe I've got the whole thing wrong. Maybe blue is for losers—like the Purple Heart.

Old Blue, a dog, has never been asked to a dog show. He just hangs around the A & P. The reason he is called Old Blue is because he is old and some eighth-graders painted him blue. Old Blue gets into people's cars and won't get out. You have to take him home with you and coax him out of your car with a T-bone steak or a filet mignon (he won't budge for hamburger).

Old Blue has a leather collar around his saggy neck with his license tag which reads: "My name is

Old Blue—please call 866-4562." When you call 866-4562 an annoyed voice asks, "Has he been fed?" If he has, then, and *only* then, will his owners send a taxi for him.

I haven't seen Old Blue in quite some time now, so I asked one of my sober neighbors what had happened to him, and he told me that Old Blue doesn't hang around the A & P these days. Some *seventh*-graders got hold of him and painted him a different color, so he doesn't have to beg anymore —he's on relief.

Almost everyone in Old New Litchridge has a dog, and some have three or four. Old New Litchridge has a leash law, which sternly warns that every dog in Old New Litchridge must be kept in a fenced yard or on a leash. So far, the Old New Litchridge Pet Shoppe and Bowwow Boutique, which was established in 1669 by some homosexuals who had fled from Fire Island to escape religious persecution, has never sold *any* leashes to *anyone*. Actually, Charles Firthby and Alden Weems and Googie Fineshriber, descendants of the original owners, confide that they'd rather *not* sell any leashes because they don't believe anything should be confined. I said, "What about a wild stallion running loose?" And Googie said, "Just leave her alone, she'll come home." (Googie is the fat one who was once guest cherub at the Botticelli festival.) The other two—Charles and Alden—look like Vic Tanny and talk like baby crows.

The dogs of Old New Litchridge run free. Free to chase cars, cats, or anything else that moves. The only time a leash is used is when some dog lover takes her pet down to Gristede's to pee on the fresh vegetables. Gristede's has the freshest vegetables—for purebred dogs only. The manager of Gristede's (God rest his soul because he's not dead yet) has long given up trying to prevent this unnecessary spraying. The women who shop with their dogs are usually such good customers he just smiles when Caldoak Pitti Pat Tylon's Victor Timstopper Dinkie-poo Charlemagne Baby, a four-pound Pomeranian who has proven to be 65-percent *fluid*, lifts his aristocratic hind leg and meticulously baptizes $80 worth of newly arrived French truffles. Also he knows that if Caldoak Pitti Pat Tylon's Victor Timstopper Dinkie-poo Charlemagne's Baby did *not* season these delicacies, the gourmets of Old New Litchridge would doubt if they were imported. As established by Caldoak Pitti Pat Tylon's Victor Timstopper Dinkie-poo Charlemagne's Baby's owner, Lady Potter-Palmer-Ormsby-Ponchatrain, Caldoak Pitti Pat Tylon's Victor Timstopper Dinkie-poo Charlemagne's Baby has *never* pissed on anything domestic.

chapter 10

"The fairest flower in the garden of creation is a young mind, offering and unfolding itself to the influence of divine wisdom, as the heliotrope turns its sweet blossoms to the sun."

—*Percy Bysshe Shelley*

WHO ELSE, IN THE DARK OF ONE NIGHT, would print "Shit" on every mailbox on Jones Ridge Road from the Merritt Parkway to the New York State line?

There is no "Youth Problem" in Old New Litchridge, because everyone in town is very understanding of the present situation. So much so that last week five boys at Old New Litchridge High School were expelled because their hair was too short. This did not create much of a cry of indignation because these five boys, it was reported in the Old New Litchridge *Advertiser*, had been troublemakers right along. They were all A students and took baths.

Not only is Old New Litchridge sympathetic and tolerant toward its young people, it has done something to help them find themselves.

The Old New Litchridge Youth Center was created because teen-agers had no place to go. That was the agonized cry that went up every time any sixteen- or seventeen-year-old was caught sticking up the Old New Litchridge National Bank. "We have no place to go!" "What *else* can we do after school?"

"We have a very unhealthy situation here in Old New Litchridge," was the conclusion of Mr. Chester Doob, who lived on Mother Luke's Lane, and was president of the Old New Litchridge National Bank, and getting a little fed up with having to hit the floor every time a masked teen-ager approached the teller's cage.

"They should have a place of their own to go," said Mrs. Hamlap, the wealthiest woman in town.

"I couldn't agree with you more," said Chester Doob. (Mrs. Hamlap kept her money in the Old New Litchridge National Bank.)

" 'I couldn't agree with you more.' You know what

"That's all you ever say to me," said Mrs. Hamlap,
I think, Chester Doob, I think you are an idiot!"

"I couldn't agree with you more," said William Kelsey.

"Now wait a minute!" said Chester Doob. "*You* don't have any money in my bank! Now—where were we?"

"I just called you an idiot," said Mrs. Hamlap.

"I couldn't agree with you more," said Chester Doob.

"How about a youth center?" said Herb Cameron.

"What?" said Mrs. Hamlap.

"A *youth center* for the kids—someplace they can twist and watusi and slop and frug and do the boogaloo."

"Mr. Cameron," said Mrs. Hamlap, speaking through Novacain lips, "there's all too much of that going on *now!*"

"I couldn't agree with you more," said Chester Doob.

"Shut up," said Herb Cameron, who maintained an irritatingly low balance in the Old New Litchridge National Bank.

"I think a youth center might be the answer," said Mrs. Hamlap, "to keep them occupied and happy. We could have a jukebox with all of the latest Lawrence Welk and Clyde McCloy hits. And maybe a Coke machine."

"How about a gumball machine?" said Herb Cameron. "That would make them *delirious!*"

Mrs. Hamlap did not react.

"*You* know," said Herb, "a *gumball machine*. You put in a penny and push the plunger and you *never* know which gumball you're going to get. It's *loads* of fun."

"Mr. Cameron," said Mrs. Hamlap, "we were speaking of a youth center, not a Barbary Coast gambling hell!"

"Yes," said Mrs. Farbstitch, "we love our children."

"Why?" said Herb Cameron.

Mrs. Farbstitch had to think.

"That's it, then," said Mrs. Hamlap. "A youth center. And we've got to give it some cute, trick name to attract them."

"How about the Coke à Go Go?" said Chester Doob.

"How about the Go Go à Go Go?" said Townsend Chichester.

"Or the Persian Room?" said Mrs. Farbstitch.

"Why?" said Herb Cameron.

Mrs. Farbstitch had to think.

"Let's give it a name that tells the whole story," said Mrs. Hamlap.

"Acne à Go Go," said Herb Cameron.

"Mr. Cameron," said Mrs. Hamlap, "if my dear husband were alive he'd horsewhip you."

"If your dear husband were alive he'd horsewhip *all* of us. That's how he got his jollies. Remember?"

"I couldn't agree with you more," said Chester Doob.

"We love our children," said Mrs. Farbstitch.

The Old New Litchridge Youth Center opened every night at 6:30 and closed at the witching hour of 9:00. This closing hour gave some of the "City Fathers" some concern, but as old Judge Crandall pointed out, "You're only young once"—which gave the other "City Fathers" a good chuckle, so they let the nine o'clock closing stand.

Being a civic-minded citizen, I asked a group of teen-agers who were hanging around in front of Cody's ice-cream store one afternoon, "How's the youth center working out?"

"What's *that?*" said one tight-blue-jeaned sheep dog.

"You know," I said, "the place where you guys go to have fun every night."

"He means up in back of the old cemetery," said another sheep dog.

"You mean they moved it?" I said.

"Naw—they didn't move it. Once they got a cemetery they leave it—they never move it."

"Yeah," said a third sheep dog, "it takes a helluva long time to move a cemetery. We know."

"You don't mean—?" I said.

"Why not?" said the second sheep dog.

"We moved every goddamn one of the stones from the old Crissy graveyard from up on the top of Huckleberry Hill," said the first sheep dog, reverently.

"Why?" I said.

"*You'll* never know," said the second sheep dog. "No one over thirty will *ever* know."

"What did you do—with this graveyard?" I said.

"You'll only laugh if we tell you," said the first sheep dog.

"No, I won't, I promise."

"Yes, you will," said the third sheep dog. Then the whole group moved up the street to strip a brand-new sports car. Myron, the cop, watched them for a while, but he couldn't do anything because they were teen-agers, and the felony they were committing was only a misdemeanor, until they reached twenty-one and they could vote and perform jury duty.

I forgot about the stolen graveyard and the missing gravestones until that spring when the snow started to melt off our patio. Then it all came back to me. I looked down one morning and there neatly inlaid among the flagstones was a mossy granite slab. The stone-carved inscription read:

MOTHER
Sarah-Ann Crissy
65 yrs. 3 mos. 2 dys.

The Old New Litchridge Historical Society has no record of Sarah-Ann Crissy, but every Mother's Day I give our patio a lovely bunch of tiny purple violets and a Whitman Sampler.

The Old New Litchridge Youth Center became an instant failure and was converted into a sort of halfway house for the mentally retarded. The Lawrence Welk recordings kept them quiet for hours, and they loved to play the gumball machine. "It's just like Las Vegas," said one retired high-school teacher, her eyes looking north and north-northwest at the same time. (She had retired after one week at Old New Litchridge High.)

But even though the youth center hadn't made the teen-ager feel *wanted*, the good citizens of Old New Litchridge didn't quit. They knew they had to give the youth of the town something to interest them and keep them out of mischief, so special events for special occasions some felt was the answer.

"The devil finds work for idle hands," said Old Judge Crandall, which didn't get much of a chuckle this time.

Halloween had been getting out of control for years, so the crafty merchants of Old New Litchridge, in order to protect their plate-glass windows against tasteless and inartistic soaping, offered a prize for the best soap design, or a soap painting. This kept most of the younger set busy on this night, and exactly at midnight the prize for the best soaped window was awarded, whereupon the losers, promptly at three minutes after midnight, tossed bricks through every other plate-glass window in the Old New Litchridge shopping area.

"The Lord giveth and the Lord taketh away," said Old Judge Crandall. Halloween always made him remember the best lines from old Judge Hardy movies.

Last Halloween the crafty store owners appealed to the *parents*, and urged *them* to supervise the window soaping contest—which they did. And as soon as the winner was announced, the parents of the losers tossed bricks through all the other plate-glass windows in the downtown shopping district.

The store owners of Old New Litchridge will never learn—"Once a Customer—Always an Enemy."

Last summer the voters of Old New Litchridge did little to cement cordial relations between the youth of the community and the people who feed them. In order to make Old New Litchridge the neat and tidy little old New England town that it is supposed to be, they bought several huge mobile vacuum cleaners. These gargantuan machines are mounted on the backs of ten-ton trucks, and every Monday morning they start cruising all the back and main roads of the town, sucking up beer cans, pop cans, dead leaves, empty cigarette packages, and retired contraceptives.

This "Operation Suck-up" has had the right impact on the appearance of the town. The roads are much neater, and these machines are holding their own against the avalanche of disposables found each morning. But there have been some untoward incidents along Héloïse and Abélard Lane in back of the old Huckleberry Hill Cemetery. Several young couples have been inhaled by these giant vacuum cleaners, which makes it very inconvenient for their parents. They have to make a special trip to the town dump to sort out their children from the rest of the debris. Some of the more astute parents forget about the children and fill the backs of their station wagons with debris, which they take home and make fascinating lamp bases out of. This sounds a little callous, but if you consider for a moment: Would *children* make fascinating lamp-bases? Dr. Strangelove and I think not.

Héloïse and Abélard Lane in back of the old Huckleberry Hill Cemetery notwithstanding, sex education is compulsory at Old New Litchridge High School. It's a very popular course, and most of the pregnant girls get a big kick out of it. Here I am giving the wrong impression again—actually there are very few unwed mothers at Old New Litchridge High. And most of them are engaged. The condition of these girls is of their own doing, with some outside help, of course, but this does not *have* to be. In the Old New Litchridge High cafeteria *every girl* has a *choice*—dessert or the pill.

Old New Litchridge is much more tolerant now than it was back in 1641. This is the information whispered to me by Miss Alma Krutch who has been doing research for years on this subject. Miss Krutch, in the comparative seclusion of the Karen Horney room at the Old New Litchridge Historical Society headquarters, confided furtively that from 1641 to 1953 an adultress would have to wear a big red *A* painted across her chest. Miss Krutch added, with slight intimation of pride, that Old New Litchridge had been the first town in New England to brand additional adultresses with the *rest* of the letters—all the way from *A* to Z. So that in a *good* year, the youngsters of Old New Litchridge learned their alphabets in no time at all. Even in a bad year in Darien.

Today there is very little of this bosom graffiti in New England, except in the hill sections of Westport, where they have no educational television.

Old New Litchridge has come a long way since 1641, in the moderation department. The Betty Boop Bottle and Boutique Shoppe features maternity wedding gowns, and during the ceremony at most of the Old New Litchridge churches, the minister wears emergency rubber gloves. And the choir is sterilized. Also, the ever-popular "Oh, Promise Me" has been replaced by "Get Me to the Church on Time."

A time-honored Outer Suburbia puberty rite deserves a passing mention. When a child reaches his sixteenth birthday, a sort of High Communion ceremony is held. The sixteen-year-old recipient is given a consecrated English muffin and a sip of tomato juice, which symbolizes the flesh and blood of Henry Ford, then he is presented with the supreme manifestation of his becoming of age, a brand-new, shiny, fast, loud automobile.

If a child reaches his sixteenth birthday *without* being given an automobile, it is believed that he will immediately become introverted and go through life with his face hidden under his armpit, or he will become an arsonist, or start wetting his bed again.

A newcomer to Old New Litchridge is in for many surprises, not the least of which are huge white footprints seen along its roads. These prints are at least as long as a car and much too large to be laughed off as belonging to someone's Jamaican housemaid who wears space shoes. When I cautiously inquired about the origin of these monstrous impressions, everyone laughed and said they were made by teen-agers—they painted them on the roads during the night. I didn't laugh and neither did they much, after I told them that, after months and months of investigation, I had found no one who had ever seen *any* teen-ager painting these gigantic footprints. And through my CIA connections at Old New Litchridge High, I learned that no one there had done this.

These footprints occur time after time on the road in front of our house and I've spent many long nights sitting at my bedroom window with binoculars but although I never see anything, the next morning these mighty footprints are there. It's as if during the darkness some ghostly wounded monster, bleeding white blood, had crossed the road on his way to some hidden haven, deep in the gloom of some still undiscovered prehistoric cave, back in what is left of the forest primeval. I knew then the alarming truth. Our house had been built right in the middle of an Abominable Snowman crossing.

I have never been able to get anyone to believe in the existence of these creatures. "You have no proof," they always say. But they're wrong. There is proof—at least proof that they once existed. Because their widows are alive and well and selling real estate in Old New Litchridge.

chapter 11

*BUNKY IS A KID WHO LIVES IN THE NEIGH*borhood. This is a supposition. He may not be a kid who lives in the neighborhood. He may just be a leprechaun who lives in a hollow tree with the old hooty owl. And how he gets in the house, we'll never know. We look around, and he's there, solemnly staring at us, his light blue eyes, with their stationary lids, never changing expression. The first time Bunky surprised us his first words were: "If you want to talk to an eagle—just get an eagle."

"Who are you?" I said.

"I'm Bunky."

"Where do you live?"

"Over there," he said, pointing at everywhere.

I said, "Oh." Then, "This is Bobby." And Bobby immediately ran to his mother. The way Bunky looked at us I wanted to do the same thing. Then, in order to make him feel at home and perhaps get Bobby to release his grip on Reiko, I said brilliantly, "What do you wanna be when you grow up?"

He said, "A bloodsucker."

I said, "You wanna watch television?"

He said, "Don't you wanna know why I wanna be a bloodsucker when I grow up?"

Bobby said, "*I* do."

Then Reiko said, "Bobby, you'll have bad dreams tonight."

I said, "What about me?"

And she said, "We're going to have spaghetti and meatballs for dinner."

Then Bobby said to Reiko, "Mommie, you know what I wanna be when I grow up— a bloodsucker."

Reiko said, "Wouldn't you rather have spaghetti and meatballs?"

"I would," said Bunky.

I said, "Okay—but we'd better call your mother and tell her you're eating with us. Do you know your telephone number?"

He said, "No, but we're on Channel Nine."

I said, "What's your last name? I'll look your phone number up in the book."

Bunky said, "I'm a guest."

I said, "Yes, that's right, but—"

He continued, "Guests can do anything they want except make loud noise."

Bobby is something like Bunky, except that we know who his parents are. One day after his fifth Christmas when Santa had brought him a real wristwatch that really ticked and the hands moved and everything, I became slightly annoyed with him because, although I get up at 5:00 A.M. in order to work, he gets up about fifteen minutes later in order to get in a full day of play, which he starts by using the top of my desk as a base for his vast fleet of jet airplanes. The sonic boom, furnished by Bobby, is almost unbearable when I'm trying to write a tender story of the love of a humpbacked midget and a spastic flower child (for Off-Broadway).

On this particular day I became so irritated, I said, "You know what I'm going to do, Bobby—I'm going to exchange you for a girl!"

He stopped a 727 jet takeoff in midair and sneered, "She won't have a wristwatch!"

Before I answered *this*, I tried to remember from Dr. Haim Ginott's book *Between Parent and Child* (New Solutions to Old Problems) just what I should say. I remembered some of the things you shouldn't say, to quote Dr. Ginott, like: "You are a disgrace to your school and no credit to your family!" or "You will end up in a federal penitentiary, that's where you'll end up!" or "If you don't settle down and stop flying those goddamn airplanes in front of my face while I'm sitting at my desk working you can forget about your allowance for this week—and next week, too! Those are the things one shouldn't say and I'm sorry, because they seem so appropriate and comforting. To me.

On another icy morning in late January, I was hunched over my old, old, old, Remington portable (it's so old the *s*'s come out *f*'s). I thought this was to be my lucky morning because Bobby had not shown up. I was working in peace and relative quiet, except for the howling wind, which seemed to be testing our picture windows' tensile strength. This placid situation was not to last. No sooner had I lost myself in the writer's enforced dream world when Bobby thumped into my life with his size 18 sneakers. He was tearing the clothes off an almost life-sized Captain Marvel plastic doll.

"What the hell are you doing?!!!" I screamed, in my best Father-of-the-Year voice.

"Shut up!" he said.

Slipping my machete out of my belt, I said, "You are a disgrace to your school and no credit to your family!"

"Shut up," he said.

I said, "Look you little—devil—one more 'shut up' and I'll cut your heart out!"

Then he looked up at me with his big brown eyes and said, "Papa, I'm glad you don't go to New York to work every day. I like it when you stay home all the time."

I said, "Okay. Okay. Now what in the hell are you doing to Captain Marvel? Why did you rip all of his clothes off?"

"I'm gonna play Jesus and Captain Marvel is gonna be Jesus."

"I thought you liked Captain Marvel the way he was."

"I do," he said, "but Jesus is better than Captain Marvel. That's what Bunky said."

"Oh," I said. "Where does Bunky get all of this inside information?"

"*Time* magazine."

"What?"

"That's what Bunky said."

Most of the children in our neighborhood seem well behaved enough except for Charlie and Madge's seven- and nine-years-olds, Durward and Googie. They look like two angels from heaven, with their long blond curls and their baby blue innocent eyes, but they are terrors. They have set their own house on fire countless times and have been, I heard, the reason for the Old New Litchridge Volunteer Fire Department losing too many members to other hobbies.

Durward and Googie's arsonist activities seem to be limited to their own home—on the outside their specialty is empty houses, or houses under construction. They are drawn like unwary sailors to the Lorelei of unbroken windows. This, Durward and Googie feel, is an intolerable condition. Windows were made to be broken. And broken they are. Such is their fascination with this type of destruction, I'm sure it will become a fetish, and in later years when they hop into bed with some willing female, they'll take a quick glance around for an unbroken window, and their lovemaking may be slightly handicapped by a rock in each hand—ready for the climactic moment.

Durward and Googie are picked up regularly by the cops and always admit readily that they have broken windows, stolen bicycles, canoes or fishing poles, or have exploded firecrackers in Old Lady Penrose's garbage can just as she was bending over to flick an aphid off her lilies of the valley. There is nothing that can be done with this pair until they are sixteen, and most of Old New Litchridge's police officers are marking off the days on the walls of their locker room—like the Count of Monte Cristo.

Bobby and *every* kid in town are at their worst

at the A & P. There is just too much to grab, and they take full advantage. There isn't a mother who hasn't arrived at the check-out counter not to be made aghast at the armful of goodies her dear little one has snatched on the way. Crackerjacks, Baby Ruths, plastic bags full of lollipops, miniature cars, tiny airplanes, midget prehistoric monsters, assorted dolls, nonassorted dolls, jelly beans, plastic pinwheels gumballs, silly putty, sober putty, half-eaten boxes of Animal Crackers, and, sometimes for the more erudite, a movie magazine or two.

The mother at this time has two choices: Let the child *keep* its purloined prizes, *return* everything to its proper section, or *shoot* the child right between the eyes and claim temporary sanity. Better make that *three* choices.

Most mothers start their children on the road to juvenile delinquency right at the A & P. They let the little darlings keep the loot and gladly (more or less) pay for it. Bobby has yet to come from there without some little trinket to show him we love him.

Bunky came home from the A & P one day with a fifteen-pound smoked ham. We found this out from him long after. When I asked him why he wanted a fifteen-pound smoked ham, he said because he had nobody to play with. He calls it Shirley. There may be more to Bunky than meets the eye. I have a feeling that someday Bunky will become even more successful than the Boston Strangler. With branch offices in Lexington, Concord, Zanesville, Ohio, and Paris, France.

Bunky isn't the only genius in our neighborhood. Bobby has shown some signs of above-average imagination. I have a small Saudi Arabian flag hanging in my office, a souvenir of a visit to Abdul's East, a tiny East Side (NYC) restaurant whose specialty was chocolate-covered sheep eyes, which are considered to be a great delicacy anywhere east of Baghdad. This Saudi Arabian flag has always fascinated Bobby because of the Arabic lettering and the large curved

Oriental sword on it. One day, he could contain himself no longer. "Papa," he said, "what kind of flag is that—American?" I said, "No—guess again." He said, "Stamford?" I didn't have the heart to say no. Also, I couldn't be so sure.

Bobby, like all children, uses our language to suit his purpose, an art which we lose forever after we have learned, or have been told thousands of times, the limitations inside of which we are supposed to stay. He, almost since he first learned to talk, has called me "Papa-boy." After a while he called Reiko "Mamma-boy." And during the summer the little playmates he finds while digging in the dirt are called "Worm-boy."

But children are very nice to have if you want to know something about your neighbors. All you have to do is invite *their* children over to play with *yours*, and what they don't volunteer you can find out by a few chosen queries like, "Does your father go to work in New York every day?" "What kind of car do you have?" "Do you have many parties at your house?" "Do you have a mortgage?" Very few are able to answer this last, but most kids being stool pigeons at heart, with their morning milk well laced with truth serum, they just love to spill their guts. Actually this kind of thing is dirty pool, and as much as I'd like to know what the hell does go with some of our more exotic near-friends, I abstain—except on rare occasions when on the day somebody new moves into the neighborhood, and I casually notice (through my 70-power binoculars) the arrival of a tall dark man wearing long white flowing robes and very black sunglasses followed by thirty-five or forty veiled women riding camels. I don't have to be told that here is a guy who has it *made*. Either that or we're in for a long, hard winter of costume parties.

chapter 12

A YEAR OR SO AGO, SWEDEN SWITCHED ITS driving from the left-hand side of the road to the right-hand side, leaving only three places in the world still driving on the left: England, Japan, and Old New Litchridge.

"Where you in church last Sunday?" said Herb Cameron, who had stopped by for a quick quart.

"No," I said.

"You shoulda been. The Reverend Henry Davies put on an illustrative pageant."

"You mean demonstrating the evils of drink?"

"Naw, he gave up on that one. Besides, everybody was getting goddamn sick and tired of seeing it. Old Dan Hooker and Old Virgil Clapham half drunk up there in the pulpit, showing everybody how booze wrecked their lives. It was ridiculous. Those two old bastards gotta be eighty years old at least—and they're the richest men in town. They didn't get the message over at all." "

"Maybe I'll start going to church again," I said, "if he's not going to do that broken-down sketch anymore. I was getting pretty sick of it myself."

"Too bad you missed last Sunday," said Herb. "The Reverend Davies really outdid himself. He staged a headon collision between two women drivers on a special platform in front of the altar, with real cars and two actual women drivers—Ruthie Howe and Mary-Ann Mulvey."

"Where the hell did he get *that* idea?" I said.

"From the Radio City Music Hall Christmas show. I saw it myself," Herb said. "It's the finale, right after the three Wise Men discover Jesus in the manger and the Rockettes do a tap dance to 'Silent

Night,' these two cars have a head-on collision. What a finish! *I* woke up."

I could see that this was going to be a long session, so I said, "Herb, I've got work to do. I gotta finish my new play."

"*This* may give you an *idea,*" said Herb. "Listen, picture if you will right in front of the altar of the Old West Church, two automobiles crashing head on! Front ends crumple. The cars shooting steam from their ruptured radiators, windshields shattered. It's sheer catastrophe. Then, after a dramatic silence, the choir starts to sing softly a new hymn by the Animals: 'Good-bye Hotrod Baby, I'll See You at That Big Drag Race in the Sky.' "

"Look, Herb," I try to say, "I've got work to do."

"Don't you wanna know what happened to the drivers—Ruthie Howe and Mary-Ann Mulvey?" Be fore I could answer, he continued, "Well, Ruthie Howe lost most of her front teeth and Mary-Ann Mulvey, she starts floating upward toward heaven."

"What???"

"She's on a rope. The Reverend Davies had it all figured out."

"Good for him."

"But the rope broke. Which was all right because the rope had been donated."

"What about Mary-Ann Mulvey?"

"Well," said Herb, "that's the sad part. It could only happen once in a *million times.*"

"For Godsakes what happened?"

"She fell into the fountain of holy water and was drowned. Actually it was a much better show than they ever put on at Radio City Music Hall—more authentic. They *never* had a *real* drowning onstage at Radio City."

"Come on," I said. "Herb—why do you make up these fantastic stories? There was nothing in the paper about anybody drowning at the Old West Church."

"Well," said Herb, "Mary-Ann Mulvey didn't *ac-*

tually drown. The Reverend Henry Davies gave her mouth-to-mouth resuscitation—which was unfortunate. He got excommunicated."

"Excommunicated!"

"Yeah," said Herb, "Bishop Mulvey came in and caught him at it."

"But he was trying to breathe life into her," I said.

"I know," said Herb, "but the bishop figured the Reverend Davies didn't have to take off her bra."

"Herb," I said, "go away. Come again some other day."

In a few moments there was a door slam and I heard horses' hooves galloping off across our lawn. Suddenly I felt sorry for Herb as I peeked out from behind a cautiously parted curtain and watched him disappear into the haze of the waning day. He seemed like such a lonely and forlorn creature—always riding his horse lonely and forlornly across people's lawns, but then I thought back to the days before he lost his driver's license, when he used to drive his *car* across people's lawns, and I felt better.

Apparently only the *women* of Old New Litchridge drive automobiles. That is, I assume they are women. It's difficult to tell. Early in the morning most of them look like Humphrey Bogart, with a head full of curlers, driving the getaway car after the St. Valentine's Day Massacre. The dead body in the seat next to them is the husband being driven to the station.

I think if the facts were known they would reveal that every woman with a car in Old New Litchridge is an ex-member of Happy Hardnose's Hell Drivers. They drive at fantastic speeds, and all on instruments. I've never seen any female actually *look* at the road while she's careening along. She's much too busy group-slapping her carpool children and at the same time trying to keep a Newfoundland dog from wrapping his paws around her neck while she's dreaming of Le Mans.

The speed limit on the narrow winding roads of Old New Litchridge is thirty-five miles per hour, and it is carefully observed only by children on tricycles. The women ignore this restriction and cruise at fifty, and sometimes break the sound barrier if they want to pass the school bus. But in all fairness I must admit they do take precautions. Almost every one of them has a neon Jesus glued over the dashboard. Even then—during the morning dash to the railroad station—St. Christopher puts on extra help. The female driver's philosophy is that any ride to the station that you can walk away from is a good ride. The ride home from the station at night can be just as hairy—perhaps hairier. They've all got a roast in the oven, and the timer isn't working.

I bear the brunt of all the weird and wild driving here because I don't commute. I work at home, and any driving I do is to the YMCA for my daily half-lap swim or to the hardware store for more floating balls for the toilets. I drive at a comfortable fifteen miles per hour, cautiously blowing my horn at every side road and hidden driveway. This helps not a bit. These leopard-women lie in wait, and as soon as I am within pouncing range, the vegetation parts in places where no hidden driveway or side road existed before and, with a terrifying roar, an infernal machine screams out of ambush, grazes my cringing fenders, and rockets down the road in front of me. The smell of cordite fills the air. I get out of my car and join a roadside elm—lifting my leafy arms to pray.

All the station wagons driven by women in Old New Litchridge seem to have a standard piece of equipment—a *large steel cage* in the rear section.

What the hell are these cages for??? *Nobody* seems to know. I can't accept Herb Cameron's theory—he says they're delivering apes.

Maybe these cages are carried in case the Newfoundland dog goes mad. Or *Junior* starts frothing at the mouth on the way to kindergarten. If the cage were portable it could be unloaded and he wouldn't have to miss a day of school—so long as the teacher keeps the other children from petting him.

Another standard accouterment for the standard Old New Litchridge female (?) driver is the lighted cigarette dangling from the side of the mouth. It never leaves there. I'm sure they smoke a special brand with epoxy tips.

Rain or snow or sleet seems to bring out the competitive spirit in these suburban Furies. They set their windshield wipers for "Geronimo!" and press the gas pedal to the floor, and it's off we go into the wild blue yonder!

Strangely enough, they always drive a lot faster when the back end of their suburban cattle trucks are filled with screaming kids. Somewhere deep within their mysterious feminine psyche must be the *idée fixe* that if they drive the front fast enough the tail will drop off like a lizard's and then they can grow a new tail—but between tails there will be *peace*. Lovely, soothing, spirit-restoring peace. But, sadly enough, this never happens—the unfortunate women of Old New Litchridge are never between tails.

The most dangerous place in all of Old New Litchridge, because of this mysterious feminine psyche, is the parking lot at the A & P. The average life expectancy of a shopping cart within its confines is about three days. Pedestrians don't last anywhere near that long.

The A & P itself is known locally as Fort Courage, and *Life* photographers assigned to cover this area have refused. The local blood bank has a permanent mobile unit here (to pick up). And there has been talk of maybe a small chapel at the entrance where a few prayers may be intoned before embarking on the great adventure, and also maybe a priest stationed at the exit—or, if that is not practical, a small religious jukebox with a recording of the last rites.

chapter 13

WHEN WE FIRST MOVED TO OLD NEW Litchridge some four years ago, we thought we would be escaping the almost daily burglaries at the Majestical House in New York's East Sixties. The Majestical House was de luxe in every sense of the word, including the price of an apartment—if not in service. There were doormen, elevator men, garagemen, security guards, and burglar alarms on all outside doors (which were disconnected during the day because the bells irritated the cleaning men). These burglar alarms were disconnected the day a burglary occurred just one apartment over from us. The thieves apparently had gone up to the roof through an inside fire escape, out through a disconnected burglar-alarm door and onto the roof, where they calmly lowered themselves to a balcony and walked into an unoccupied apartment through the French doors, which the owners were naïve enough not to lock because they never expected visitors from the burglar-alarmed roof-top.

The intruders made off with a few thousand dollars' worth of jewelry and furs. The furs they threw off the balcony to the street twenty floors below, where they were caught by a confederate and neatly piled in the back of a waiting car. In New York this particular caper would not rate a flicker of an eyelash from anyone who had witnessed it. In fact, anywhere on any street in New York, thirty-five men dressed as Boy Scouts could gang rape a zebra, and nobody would give it a thought—except maybe another zebra.

New York's crime is mostly racial—black, brown,

yellow, white, or lavender—and is caused by too many people living in slums near a liquor store.

Old ladies are now mugging teen-agers and old men are buying Jekyll and Hyde kits and hanging around the back door to the YWCA (where the scrubwomen come out). On television and radio, the police commissioner keeps admonishing anyone who will listen: "Don't leave your car keys in your car—keep them in a safe-deposit box!"

Crime is rampant in the Greenwich Village area where runaway girls, who are given generous allowances at home, come to panhandle.

Murder, rape, assault, and burglary are something to be lived with in New York. But not by us. This is the city from which we fled to the calm and comfort and safety of the suburbs.

The first week we lived in Old New Litchridge, after a getting-to-know-you dinner with the chief of police, we arrived home to discover that we had been burglarized.

These suburban thieves must have been an odd lot because all they took were two large cartons of old Lum and Abner radio scripts, which are worth very little to anyone outside of a collector of old Lum and Abner radio scripts—or large cartons.

After this unexpected contact with local crime, we bought the two Doberman pinschers, who had been trained to attack on command. Evidently we had been given the wrong command, because whatever we said to them during an emergency such as tiny tots selling Girl Scout cookies, they reacted as if we had given the order to *mix*. Everyone and anyone who entered our front yard was smothered with love and kisses, and escorted to the front door like visiting royalty. Later we found out *who* they were trained to attack on command. *Us*. They resented any kind of discipline, and when we realized that they considered themselves house guests and not servants, peace and tranquillity once more settled down over Sunnybrook Farm.

When we first moved here most of the neighbors airily informed us that they never locked their doors when they left the house. Later, during a Martini break, they confessed that they had been stolen blind. Some people had lost whole rooms full of furniture, and one trusting old gentleman had had his entire collection of ancient Turkish dueling swords stolen—one of which turned up some two weeks later when a newly emigrated Puerto Rican tried to hold up a liquor store in Stamford. This poor misguided would-be criminal walked into Louie's Liquor Store on High Ridge Road and said: "*En garde!* This is a stickup!" Louie, who happens to be of Turkish extraction, picked up *his* ancient Turkish dueling sword which he kept under the counter in case somebody walked in and attacked him with an ancient Turkish dueling sword. The whole episode ended in tragedy. The nervous Puerto Rican was so startled at Louie's choice of weapon that he inadvertently stabbed himself, and Louie, in his anxiety to prove that he was Turkish, swung at the intruder and lopped off his brother-in-law's left ear. It was, on the whole, a most unsatisfactory attempted crime. The police, after advising the bleeding Puerto Rican of his new legal rights, arrested him for stabbing a Puerto Rican. They also arrested Louie for illegal possession of his brother-in-law's left ear, which he had been trying to Scotch Tape back on when the officers arrived at the store.

Louie's brother-in-law was fairly lucky. A famous Greenwich doctor who specializes in ear transplants took an ear from a recent accident victim and sewed it on Louie's brother-in-law. The fact that it is a female ear bothers him not at all, but his wife, Mabel, grateful as she is to the Greenwich doctor, sometimes wishes that the doctor had removed the pearl pendant earring first. And so do the rest of the fellows in his National Guard unit.

We are regularly visited here in Old New Litchridge by apprentice junkies, who come to the door on the pretext of looking for someone else who lives in the neighborhood. Or they want to know if we'd like a subscription to *Collier's*. Or would we care to send a Care package to the Perth Amboy natives. Then again we get someone who is working his way through ballet school, and would like a few dollars for fingernail hardener. All these nutty subterfuges are, of course, obvious cover-ups for their real mission—which is to break into and burglarize your house. And if no one answered the door, this is exactly what would happen. And until junk comes down in price, we are going to have these unwelcome visitors *ad infinitum*. And as a result, contrary to the wishes of our good Senator Dodd, we are fully armed. We are so fully armed that at times I feel we may be hampering the war effort. Reiko has a .38 Smith & Wesson police special, I have a Colt .45 automatic, and Bobby has a single-shot .22. And we have been taking lessons from a shooting instructor named Buggsy Murdock. Buggsy is always in the process of being put on parole or breaking it. He's never static. Our little family is getting quite proficient in the art of suburban defense, and I'm reasonably sure that, if we are invaded some dark night or bright morning, somebody is going to get hurt. Could be us.

There are many types of defense now being used against the suburban crime wave. The rich, of course, have moats—filled with piranha, the tiny but voracious South American fish, who can strip the flesh from a 1,200-pound ox in fifteen seconds. The rich are *ready*—in case of an attempted burglary by a 1,200-pound ox.

This type of defense is not too practical, of course, in winter when the moat freezes over and the 1,200-pound ox knows how to skate.

The middle-income groups have their own methods to combat the vast hordes of TV set thieves. Most families have a dog. And even the smallest bark of the smallest dog will discourage unwanted visitors, according to the police. Herb Cameron bought a dog for this purpose, but his house was burglarized six times in two months. When I asked him what kind of a dog he'd bought, he said it was given to him by a friend who had brought it from Africa, and it is called a Basenji, which my dog pediatrician informs me is barkless. When I told Herb about this, he rushed right out and bought a bloodhound, whom, in case of a break-in, the Basenji nudges into a semi-alert and the bloodhound yelps a few times and the crisis is averted. Herb's only complaint is that the bloodhound is getting too fat from lying around doing nothing. He was seriously considering moving close to some nearby prison honor farm and paying one of the inmates to escape every other week. I saw Herb recently and his scheme hasn't worked out. It seems he can't find a good prison honor farm close enough to a good golf course, which to me is extremely odd in this day of enlightened prison reform and rehabilitation.

The suburban criminal is the boldest in the world. Fifty-foot trees have been excavated from front lawns, loaded on trucks, and sold to someone in Greenwich or Bronxville or, in order to cut the hauling charge, to the neighbors *next door!*

One morning last spring the Old New Litchridge railroad station was found a half mile from the railroad. This was most unusual and the chief of police attributed the theft to some railroad buff. After it happened again last summer, it was put on a leash. If this seems like an exaggeration—it is.

Ninety pistols were taken one night from John's Sports. The Daughters of the American Teen-ager, a local organization dedicated to the pregnant youth of Old New Litchridge, was put on record as saying that *this* was further proof that the frustrated youth of today is trying to *express* itself by making itself *noticed.* This statement turned out to be true. Ninety teen-agers sticking up Westport was mentioned *quite prominently* in the Westport papers.

The young aren't the only group that dabbles in crime. A few summers ago two male schoolteachers turned to housebreaking to finance a pilgrimage to Mecca. When the judge asked them, "Why Mecca?" they said, "We've *been* to the Virgin Islands."

For months, last year, Old New Litchridge was plagued by a so-called "Cat Burglar." Why he was called the "Cat Burglar" I've never been able to fathom, but when he was apprehended it turned out that he was the driver of the airport bus. He would drive you to the airport, then come back and rob your house. It was a perfect system until one midnight he foolishly made the mistake of creeping into the Victorian mansion of Miss Rose Van Lennep, an eighty-three-year-old spinster, who slept the sleep of pristine innocence in a delicately curved Hepplewhite fourposter, surrounded on all four sides by ingeniously placed bear traps.

Sometime after this the Cat Burglar became the "Wheelchair Burglar" and robbed only ranch houses. Or split levels with ramps.

Suburbia's main crime problem is juvenile vandalism. Mailboxes are the chief target and are treated in one of three ways. A stranger driving down a country road might be shocked and startled by the four-letter names of the families living in the residential areas—according to the mailboxes. Also they might be intrigued by the duplication of names. Some mornings Old New Litchridge seems to be populated by only three families.

Many other crushingly clever pranks are perpetrated by the young lions of Old New Litchridge. One hardware store owner opened up on a Monday morning to find all of his accounts spread on the floor—covered with a half inch of hardened shellac. Something snapped in his mind, because he ordered more shellac and the following Monday morning his nephew discovered that he now had a mummified uncle. They're planning to place a dead canary in his hands and mount him at the entrance to the Old New Litchridge Pet Cemetery.

One wealthy family, after six weeks in Europe, returned home to discover that some fun-loving Rover Boy had unplugged their deep freeze and some 4,000 filet mignons, 3,600 lamb chops, 789 servings of frozen spaghetti, and 900 gallons of meat sauce were, to put it most delicately, uneatable. The accumulation of odors was so strong Westport thought that Darien had died.

chapter 14

NO ONE WE KNOW HAS BEEN SO CONSER-vative about children as we have. By some restraint and good old American know-how, we have kept our population explosion down to one. This is not so with our friends. All our friends are breeders. And they never miss. If I wake up some morning in the very near future and read about a worldwide shortage of peanut butter and jelly, I won't be surprised one damned bit. However, I can't play God (mainly because I haven't the correct wardrobe), so I won't try to—not until I get a few more followers. So let them have their overswarm of cherubs and order Pablum in carload lots. We'll stick to one—he's more than enough.

Artie and Phyllis Bolger, our first weekend guests, had only one child—but not an ordinary everyday run-of-the-mill child—they had a five-year-old *goddess*. This goddess, whom Artie and Phyllis, by some *miracle*, had created, turned out to be extremely brittle. Or so it seemed. Her name was Little Trishy. Every time this five-year-old divinity would get knocked on her sacred ass while playing with Bobby, Phyllis would be on the telephone trying frantically to reach the nearest emergency hospital, while Artie would be paving Little Trishy with miles of Band-Aids.

Momsie and Dadsie were so terrified that Little Trishy was going to break some integral part of her that whenever the child would run a little or even *walk* a little, they'd both scream, "Be careful, Trishy!" "Trishy—be CAREFUL!" "TRISHY!!!!!!!!!"

By late Saturday afternoon, I had had it with Artie and Phyllis but most of all I had had it with

Little Trishy, so I asked her if she would like to play Little Red Riding Hood. She said, "Yes."

Artie and Phyllis were deeply apprehensive as I slipped Trishy into a little red raincoat.

"What kinda game is this?" Artie wanted to know.

"You'll see," I said.

"I don't like Little Trishy wearing somebody else's raincoat," said Phyllis. "It's not healthy."

"You're so right," I agreed. Then I opened the porch door and let Tanuki into the living room.

"Oh, boy!" said Little Trishy. "Look, Momsie and Dadsie—a *wolf!*"

Momsie and Dadsie were no longer able to hear.

Other types of weekend guests who are hard to digest are the restless ones. They are the ones who keep saying, "Now don't you worry about us, we'll entertain ourselves. Let's take a walk. How's the fishing? How about going over to your golf club? Any sailboating around here? Horseback riding? Polo? Jai alai? Hunting? Hockey? Skeet? How about a swim? Skiing? Let's go over to your golf club—"

It hurts to have to admit that I don't belong to the Old New Litchridge Golf Club, and my guests really give me the fisheye of doubt when I tell them that the waiting list goes back to the time of William the Conqueror. Then I carefully have to explain why we can't do any of the other fun things they've planned on. No matter what I say, it still sounds as if I'm a real sonofabitchin' spoilsport. And I guess I am, but I blame it on my naïveté and innocence. I will never give up thinking that people who live in the city and spend five days a week putting up with its conveniences would like to come to the peace and quiet of the country and rest. Catch their breath. Meditate. Why must they try out for the Olympics?

Ed and Mary Ronson are the "Let's make a hernia" weekend type. Ed, whose only claim to athletic immortality is when he came in *third* in the Baby Derby at Palisades Park (he says the other mothers had cattle prods). I thought he would like to spend a weekend doing sensible things, like getting too much sun or loaded, but no—he wanted action. And for this he was really in the wrong establishment. The last time I entertained any thought along this line was a couple of years ago at Yellowstone Park when I had disregarded the warning about leaving your car to photograph the bears. Actually, I hadn't ignored the warning sign; I was just trying to do a bear a favor. He was a big brown one and he had a Polaroid and he wanted to photograph *me*. That's the way it happened. Nobody believes this story, but nobody believed Robert Fulton, or Orville and Wilbur, or Lydia Pinkham—at first.

But getting back to Ed and Mary. Along about Ed's sixth suggestion for fun, and my sixth rejection, he turned surly and immediately it started to rain. This unnerved me. Then Reiko whispered that she had forgotten to buy club soda which unnerved me even more, because I knew that Ed had finally stopped drinking Coca-Cola with his Scotch, after reading what he thought was a sex novel by Amy Vanderbilt.

Somehow we got through Friday night, Saturday, and Sunday with Ed and Mary, but I felt that Ed was about to blow. His eyes, which were none too coordinated even when life was beautiful, were starting to dart off in opposite directions, which was ideal for watching both sides during a tennis match, but sitting across from him at the dinner table, I felt like a petty officer at the Last Supper with Captain Queeg. I knew I had to do something to save his sanity—plus his weekend, so in a moment of particularly ominous silence, I suggested that when it was time for them to leave, we could have a drag race from our house to the Merritt Parkway. There was an explosion of gratitude and the next thing I knew we were screaming neck and neck down Jones Ridge Road toward the parkway.

Unfortunately, Herb Cameron and his weekend guests were drag racing in the opposite direction at the very same time. The crash could be heard for miles, but nobody was hurt and Herb had the presence of mind to say, as we were all standing around surveying the wreckage when the police drove up, "Goddamn teen-agers!"

Probably the worst type of weekend guests are the perfect ones. Everything pleases and amuses and entertains them immensely. So much so that after a while you don't believe it. John and Virginia Hall are like this. When John burst into the breakfast nook on a gloomy Saturday morning, the whole room lighted up. He said he had had the best night's sleep he had ever had. The bed was the most comfortable he had ever slept in. He loved the sheets, the pillowcases, the mattress, the mattress pad, the night light, the small volume of *Jack London's Best,* the *Gideon Bible,* the three old *National Geographics,* the bedside ashtray, the packet of Gristede's matches, the wallpaper, the Toulouse-Lautrec prints, the Hans Erni prints, the Max's Garage calendar, the imitation cashmere throw rug, the closets, the clothes hangers, the picture window, the wall thermostat, the Japanese draperies, the drawstrings. Then in the bathroom he had adored the washbowl, the toilet, the bathtub, the toothbrush holder, the Dixie Cup holder, the soap dish, the hot water, the cold water, the shaving light, the bath mat, the Handy-Dandy emergency plunger, the tile, the cracks in the tile (so authentic), the bath towels, the hand towels, and the facecloths.

Not content with well enough alone, I said, "John, there must be *something* you *didn't* like." This brought him up short but he recovered miraculously and said, "I can't think of a thing except—maybe—the toothpaste."

"The toothpaste?" I said. "What the hell's wrong with the toothpaste?"

"Well," he said, "I mean no offense, but . . . someone squeezed it from the wrong end."

"Jesus Christ!" said Bobby, who frequently imitates his articulate father.

"But," John added quickly, "*I* fixed it. I started squeezing it at the *other* end. I'm sure it will be all right now. I'm quite handy at things like that. Right, Virginia?"

"Yes," said Virginia. "He does it all the time when we're home."

"Jesus Christ!" said Bobby.

"That's enough!" I told Bobby, and he immediately burst into tears.

"You hurt his feelings," said Reiko.

"Jesus Christ!" I said.

"This is marvelous," said John. "A real family, with its joys and tears and laughter and a little sorrow, but still—a real family. A happy family."

Bobby stopped crying and Reiko stopped smoking. Virginia stopped sipping her coffee and I stopped on my way to whack Bobby. "What?" I said.

"Yeah," said John, "it's just like Ozzie and Harriet."

"Jesus Christ!" said Reiko. "What's *that*?"

John was the worst perfect weekend guest we ever had. He saw something beautiful in everything. When the guest toilet became stopped up at 3:00 A.M. Sunday morning and we needed assistance, he complimented the emergency plumber on the color of his truck. And the plumber, who ordinarily doesn't respond to cordiality, just loved John's bathrobe. John took it off and gave it to him. Then, as we all stood gratefully at the door, singing "Beyond the Reef," as the plumber was leaving—his arms piled high with bottles of liquor and other tithes and bon voyage gifts—John admired the plumber's rubber plunger. The plumber, forgetting for a moment that he was not mortal, gave it to him.

"What a beautiful human being," murmured John as the plumber clinically backed his truck over Bobby's tricycle and a priceless Japanese maple, then drove off into the cool gray dawn and his next porcelain patient.

"He's a sonofabitch!" I said.

"You may be right," agreed John.

"Sonofabitch!" said Bobby. And John agreed with him, too.

The whole weekend was getting to be too much for me. The tidal wave of sweetness and light and agreeability was about to swamp my always overloaded rowboat of tolerance. I knew I couldn't last until the 9:29 left the Old New Litchridge station on Sunday night, so I deliberately tried to provoke an argument. It was difficult, almost to the point of impossible, but not to keep you in nerve-wracking suspense, I'll tell you now—I made good. The first few tactics didn't work. I criticized his wife's hairdo. I told him *he* was too fat. I told him his Ho Chi Minh coat was too Jewish-looking. I told him his *wife* was too fat. I told him that I was sure that soon his job would be taken over by a computer. I told him I didn't like his mother's cooking. I told him I didn't like his mother. I told him that I knew his wife before he did and that she used to get drunk and stay at my apartment overnight, and that we used to read the *Karma Sutra* together on a white polar bear rug in front of a roaring fireplace with blue lights.

I said all this and nothing happened. This clown wasn't real! There was only one thing left.

"John," I said, "it may be the light, but isn't your hair getting a little thin on top?"

He punched me right in the mouth.

chapter 15

A PARTY WAS HELD ON THE JULY 4 WEEK-end here in Old New Litchridge. These are quotes from the Old New Litchridge *Advertiser*, under "Social Doings" by Gad A. Bout:

Harold Fenser of 12386 Jones Ridge held his usual Fourth of July Gala at "Hollyhock Hill," the home of his parents, Mr. and Mrs. Thomas Fenser, who are touring Europe this summer. Between 900 and 1,000 guests attended and consumed 300 barrels of beer as they danced to the music of Lester Lanin, Meyer Davis, and Monk Murk and the Offals. It was not only the Fourth of July, it was Harold Fenser's sixteenth birthday.

The party, according to the invitations, was to begin at noon on Friday and go on until the "wee small hours" of Monday or Tuesday.

Harold Fenser, an enterprising young man, charged each guest $5 as a "contribution" to his favorite charity and new furniture, which he planned to purchase before his parents, Mr. and Mrs. Thomas Fenser, who are touring Europe, return. Young Mr. Fenser also plans to have the Fenser driveway repaved. It seems that one of the guests thought it would be great fun to clear the confetti off the driveway with the Fenser snowplow, but due to his inexperience, he plowed a "mite too deep," as Tito Passantino, the Fenser gardener, explained. Mr. Passantino's parents, we learned, are planning a tour of America in the near future.

At 10:30 on Saturday night, the State Police were alerted by Captain Fred Passantino of the Old New Litchridge police. This was after some of Mr. Fenser's neighbors complained that a large detachment of German World War I soldiers were seen marching toward the party. Later reports confirmed this bizarre episode, but it was explained that they were not German soldiers, but a group of high-school students who belonged to the General von Hindenburg fan club of Fairfield County.

Complaints from more neighbors brought the police tow trucks to remove several sports cars that had been

parked on nearby lawns, driveways, garages, and in not a few swimming pools, which had been mistaken for parking lots in the bright moonlight. Shirley McKay Smith and Ralf Trusdale of South Barrington, Massachusetts, had been trapped for more than three hours in a Volkswagen at the bottom of a swimming pool on the estate of E. K. Lynch, the prominent attorney. Miss Smith and Mr. Trusdale were treated for immersion and exposure, which they later were arrested for. Mr. E. K. Lynch, the prominent attorney, does not intend to press charges but informed this reporter that Carmine Passantino, the well-known local scuba diver, had given him an estimate of $47.29 to erase the tire marks from the bottom of his swimming pool. Mr. E. K. Lynch was graduated from Harvard Law School in 1903.

Cannon fire was heard to be coming from the Fenser estate at 3:25 A.M. Sunday morning. Upon investigation, Captain Fred Passantino and Detectives Scott Passantino and Irving Passantino discovered a World War II howitzer and three bazookas, plus seven cannon, which had been used to stop the boys in blue at the Battle of Richmond. Upon being questioned about this vast store of armament, young Mr. Fenser said their possession was entirely legal and that he had purchased this armament through the mail. Captain Passatino confiscated the entire arsenal until it could be decided whether or not cannon may be discharged in Old New Litchridge on private property in time of peace.

At 6:15 A.M. thirteen young girls were seen by a next-door neighbor of Mr. Fenser's to be dancing nude on the front lawn of the estate, but when the police, under Captain Passantino, arrived, the thirteen nude girls had disappeared. When the next-door neighbor, Mr. Clyde Harper, the prominent New York banker and member of the Lions Club, was questioned by Captain Passantino, he admitted that the light had been poor and there probably weren't more than six or seven girls.

Mr. Harper was graduated from Ohio State.

The first party *we* were asked to when we first moved to Old New Litchridge was a "Welcome to Old New Litchridge Party." I don't remember having a very good time because everyone at the party acted like *he* had just moved to Old New Litchridge and didn't know who was welcoming whom to Old New Litchridge.

I was dressed in my city clothes—a black suit,

black shoes, black socks, black tie, and white tab-collared shirt. All the other men were dressed as country squires. Multicolored checked tweed coats. Red corduroy trousers and rough-textured desert boots. Their shirts were open at the collar and their necks were carefully gift wrapped in brilliant Ascot ties. Pinned with what looked like bronzed gallstone clusters. Their complexions were sunlamp ruddy, and their perfectly capped teeth flashed confidently in the late-afternoon sunshine, as the bon mots flowed like constipated lava.

"What's your game?" one of them asked me.

"Nothing," I said. "I was *asked* to come here."

"No, no," he said. "I meant—what do you do? IBM?"

"No."

"You're not—with IBM?"

"No, I write. I'm a writer." I smiled, inviting warmth.

"Oh," he said, visibly shaken. He backed away, never taking his eyes from me. Then he turned and hurried toward the bar.

"My *brother* used to be with IBM! His name is Crickard. He was an All-America at Harvard; now he's got a liquor store up in Buffalo!" I called after him, but it was too late. I'd lost him. Forever.

Wary, the next person I spoke with was a Mrs. Kling, who looked like Lee Marvin. With a voice like Shirley Temple. I volunteered that I was with IBM, and also that I was a Communist, a John Bircher, a draft dodger, an undercover agent for an unfriendly country, a wife beater, a dog hater, a butterfly murderer, and did *not* play golf. Mrs. Kling rolled back her lips, showing me far more of her gums than I ever care to see again, and said that she was very glad that I had moved to Old New Litchridge and what a pity it was that I didn't play golf.

Then we have the surprise party givers. About once every three days—or so it seems—Mr. and Mrs. Henry Blackwell give a surprise party. But only for each other. Ever since our first experience with Henry and Vivian, we have been extremely chary of them. The first party we went to was in honor of Vivian's birthday. Henry got her out of the house on the wild pretext that he was taking her to dinner. Which he did. Then the guests, after a decent interval, gathered in the backyard, where we were all supposed to lurk in the dark shadows and burst forth when Henry brought Vivian back from dinner and got her out into the backyard—on another wild pretext.

The time was early spring and not really the season to stand around in party dresses and mohair suits. Thermal underwear and mukluks would have been more appropriate. After about twenty or thirty minutes the guests, though fortified with booze, were getting restive. The reason we were all in the backyard was because we were supposed to dance on the flagstone terrace—to the music of an orchestra that hadn't arrived yet either. It began to look as if *we* were the ones who were getting surprised.

Long after the hour that anyone would be finished with dinner and several after-dinner brandies, Henry and Vivian hadn't shown up. The orchestra had, and its members turned surly when they couldn't find an electrical outlet to plug themselves in. Unplugged they sounded very soggy, but they played anyway. Everybody danced in self-defense. The temperature now hovered around freezing. After a while the hundreds of bright balloons, which were strung out through the trees and overhead, gave up and became limp, creating a clothesline of multicolored obscenity. The guests moved like a North Pole expedition that wasn't going to make it. Their attempts at dancing resembled the movements of the Black Mass. The uneven cement on the terrace floor made dancing more of an improbable task than a social grace. The effect was like trying to ski *up* Mount Everest with sandpaper skis and a sea anchor. The orchestra, which had found a hot line, now entertained themselves with *volume.* Screech owls for miles around ruined their vocal chords forever. Still no Henry and Vivian.

"Maybe," said Joe Bickley, "maybe they got so loaded they decided to spend the night in a motel."

"But they're married," said Mrs. Parker.

"Sure," said Joe, "but maybe they're so loaded they don't know each other."

"I never thought of that," said Mrs. Parker. "Sounds like fun."

"I'm gettin' outa here," said Vernon Basset. "I don't wanna surprise Vivian. I wanna surprise myself when I find out I'm still alive in the morning. Look at my drink; there's ice forming on the top of it. I don't wanna freeze to death on a lousy terrace in Connecticut. If I'm gonna freeze to death, it'll be carrying the serum to Nome and no other way."

"God bless Balto," said Mrs. Parker.

"What?" said Basset.

"I said, 'God bless Balto.' What's the matter with you, you sonofabitch, can'tcha hear???" said Mrs. Parker, spilling most of her Scotch into what she thought was her cleavage. "He was the one who carried the goddamn serum to goddamn Nome!" Then she collapsed and disappeared into a large clump of sweetheart roses.

"She's smart," said Basset, and joined her.

Henry and Vivian showed up at 11:15 P.M. Stoned. Henry, giggling like a pregnant schoolgirl, maneuvered Vivian into the backyard and pushed her toward a concrete love seat. Vivian seemed very willing, and I felt that Henry was about to give Vivian an unpremeditated odzookens for her birthday—on the concrete love seat.

It all happened so suddenly, nobody yelled, "Surprise!" but after a while there were quite a few "Bravos!"

chapter 16

I MET HERB CAMERON AT THE OLD NEW Litchridge YMCA, where we both were going daily to take the baths. When I first met Herb, who is a very successful writer and editor, I thought he was a nut. I still do. As we were changing into our swim trunks in the sweat-perfumed confines of the locker room, Herb's first words to me were, "Did you ever have a dog that looked like Sandra Dee?"

I said, "No."

Herb was quiet for a few minutes. Then after tying the strings of his swim trunks he walked over to me and said, confidentially, "Don't drink the water."

I said, "Where?"

He said, "In the pool."

I said, "What?"

He said, "Even if you're *drowning*—don't drink the water!"

There was just him and me in the locker room and I was getting a little nervous.

"Do you know where you are?" he said.

Now I wasn't so sure, but I said, "At the YMCA?"

He said, "There's more to it than that. This is one of Old New Litchridge's historical landmarks—it was built in 1961—by slave labor."

I said, "Huh?"

He said, "Yeah—they only got five fifty an hour— But we wouldn't have a YMCA in Old New Litchridge if it hadn't have been for old H. K. J. Purvis. He was the first—the *very* first IBM executive ever to settle in Old New Litchridge—way back in fifty-seven. This was the old carriage house. Old H. K. J. Purvis donated it to the town for a YMCA. While it was burning down."

"Quick thinking," I said.

"Yeah," said Herb. "Too bad he commited suicide. IBM wanted him buried at Arlington, but it didn't work out."

"Was he a veteran?" I said.

"Twenty-seven years with the firm. His wife tried all sorts of gimmicks to get him into Arlington—she wanted them to build a small white marble mausoleum and call it the 'Tomb of the Unknown IBM Executive,' but they wouldn't go for it. She even said that she'd see that H. K. J. Purvis wouldn't get any credit for being in there."

"Well," I said, "I came here to take a swim—"

This seemed to ruffle Herb a bit and he said, "You are going to take a swim in old H. K. J. Purvis' swimming pool without asking how he committed suicide?"

I said, "I didn't think it was too important—"

Herb said, "He stuck his head into one of his own computers and set it for 'Population Statistics'—but his suicide didn't count."

"Why not?" I said.

"Because the computer didn't have his Social Security number," Herb said.

The Old New Litchridge *Young* Men's *Christian* Association has neither. Outside of myself. I am the youngest member—in the swimming pool contingent anyway. Which will give you some idea of what a robust group we are. I am the only one who can swim the entire seventy-eight-foot length of the pool without a little man in a rowboat following and syphoning beef broth to me during the crossing.

The prodigious aquatic accomplishments of the other members are duly remembered with little bronzed marker plates along the sides of the pool: "Gowdy Pillens—33 feet—Aug. 12, 1962," "Newbold Sutcliffe—38 feet—Jan. 27, 1965," etc. etc. There is one tiny bronzed marker, just *one* foot short of the pool's seventy-eight-foot length, edged in black.

The clientele at the Y is divided into two fat,

breathless groups. The swimmers and the perspirers. The perspirers arrive at twelve noon each day and immediately change into sweat suits and sneakers. Then they disappear into something called the gym. In the gym they are given small doses of apoplexy and soon drag themselves back into the locker room to undress and scald themselves in the shower. The shower acts like Bela Lugosi bringing back the dead. This group, no matter how much they "exercise," never looks like anything more than part of an experiment started forty years ago in a Kentucky cave to see who could stay down there the longest. Their eyes have all the sparkle of dusty grapes and their skins glow with the pallor of an unborn newt.

I started swimming at the Y on the advice of my doctor. He told me I was too dry. He added that I swam every day for six months I would feel 1,000 percent better. At the end of six months I was about 976 percent short of feeling better, but I'm much damper, and I'm beginning to sprout ferns and lilies of the valley in the god-damnedest places.

The time allotted to the men swimmers is daily between twelve noon and one o'clock. The pool then is given over to the women swimmers from one to two. Promptly at ten minutes to one, the women come flapping out of their locker room and are properly annoyed to find that the pool hasn't been swept clean of men. Some of these flounderfooted, lardy naiads clump back into their locker room incensed from the tips of their peeling painted toes to the tops of their blue-rinsed Roman senator ringlets. Others stand around tapping their feet and looking at the watches they forgot to take off, trying to decide whether to complain to management or drop a live electric wire into the deep end of the pool. The men, ignoring this peril beyond the point of prudence, keep swimming right up until the big red second hand of the clock hits one, and the women hit the water with a viciously accusing thwack! I don't know why women are so anticipatory. Maybe they haven't much time and have to get back home to "Love of Life" and "Secret Storm" and "General Hospital."

So much for the bathing beauties of the YMCA pool. Except this: They are not, no matter what they think, Rhine Mermaids. They couldn't lure Siegfried onto the rocks if Siegfried was Harry Hardcock, the Wyoming sheepherder who herded only rams.

Kids use the Old New Litchridge Y on Saturdays. I didn't know this the first Saturday I was there and the building started to swing and sway without Sammy Kaye. Having been in on a couple of sneak previews of California earthquakes, I was sure that this was what was happening when suddenly the door of the locker room opened and in poured the advance rabble of the French Revolution.

Instantly the locker room was a shambles. Every locker was slammed open until one was found that suited each individual taste, although each locker was no different from any other locker in the room. But this apparently was part of the sacred ritual of being a small boy. The floor was now wall to wall with dirty sneakers, dirty underwear, and clean towels. Batman sweatshirts, Cub Scout shirts, and number 69 football jerseys were flung into their favorite (for that day at least) lockers. Then came the crisis. Where is my bathing suit? One out of every three kids hasn't the slightest idea what happened to his suit, although he may be holding it in his hand or standing on it. Or wearing it.

After everyone else had run screaming toward the pool, one small, forlorn little boy was left. He was sitting on one of the benches in front of the row of battered green lockers. I said, "Aren't you gonna go swimming?"

He said, "Nope, I forgot my bathing suit."

I said, "Why don't you go home and get it? Where do you live?"

He said, "My mother brought me."

I said, suddenly becoming Calvin the Compassionate, "I'll take you home, but you'd better call your mother and tell her that Mr. Douglas is going to bring you home." (I didn't want to get pinned with a kidnapping rap; besides, I don't think this kid's parents would have paid one red cent to have him returned.) "Go out front and call."

"Okay," he said. In fifteen seconds he was back. "I need a dime and I haven't got one."

"Here's a dime." He left again, and in a moment or two he was back.

"Did you call your mother?"

"She wasn't home."

"Is anybody home?"

"Yes."

"Who?"

"I dunno. I didn't need the dime to call; they let me call for nothing."

"That's good," I said. "Where's the dime?"

"I lost it."

Outside, after getting this kid strapped in the car (he had never seen a safety belt before so I had to give a twenty-minute lecture on its use before he would consent to put it on), after his qualms were qualmed and his curiosity satisfied, I got in, fastened my belt, and started the engine. "Now," I said, "where do you live?"

"There," he said, pointing to a small house right next door to the Y.

We may be living in a country where any little boy can grow up and become President of the United States, but while I'm still able to vote, I'll see that *this* kid doesn't make it.

The Old New Litchridge YMCA has an extremely comprehensive curriculum. There isn't anything you can't learn there, including Swahili, judo, and meditation. Judo is taught by a wearer of the lavender belt, which is 'way beyond the black belt. If one of his students managed to toss him on his hairdo, his lower lip would get all Jello-y like Jackie Cooper's used to when Wally Beery lost the heavyweight championship and came home drunk. Or maybe it was Jackie who came home drunk; I've forgotten. But this judo expert finally broke his wrist waving to some of the boys from the pet food store one night at Madame Egret's bar and had to quit. The last anyone ever heard of him he was in New York walking two lovely Russian wolfhounds on Third Avenue.

After this, the Y hired a karate expert who wasn't around very long after a little episode in Manny Passantino's restaurant. To demonstrate his prowess he placed a breadstick on top of two water glasses then proceeded to fracture every bone in his right hand trying to break it with a karate chop.

Then Bowman Hunter, the Y director, switched the whole program to Yoga and meditation.

The gentleman who is in charge of this department is well qualified for the teaching of Yoga. He has two broken legs and a dirty sheet. He has no trouble at all sitting like that. According to Bowman Hunter, who briefed all of us potential meditators in the locker room one day, this gamy little old man is called a guru. And that's just exactly what he looks like.

All in all I've been to nine meditation meetings, along with about a dozen other nuts who would like to communicate with somebody other than their friends or family. So far, I haven't learned very much. I could burn incense and contemplate my navel long before I ever met this guru. Herb Cameron, on the other hand, seems to have absorbed a great deal more and has advanced to a much higher plateau than the rest of us. *He* can contemplate his incense and burn his navel. *That*, Baby, is *meditation!*

chapter 17

FROM TIME TO TIME, WHEN LIFE BECOMES too much for me I hire a part-time secretary to type up scripts plus retaliatory letters to banks, insurance companies, utility companies, grass seed companies, and various other groups who have gone out of their way to irritate me. All I asked The Cohen Girls, a secretarial service in Stamford, was for someone who looked like Raquel Welch and who could take shorthand like Billy Rose. They sent me something that not only did *not* look like Raquel Welch, but before she had been here more than three minutes, I wished looked like Billy Rose. Her name was Miss Habbleburger and she brought her own sterile coat hanger to hang her sterile coat on. This was just the beginning. The typewriter she was sometimes to touch with the sterilized tips of her Lysol hands was thoroughly sprayed with DDT. My office, which I must admit, looks like it might be the central breeding ground for every known type of deadly germ, horrified this pasteurized peahen. She rummaged frantically around in her emergency immunization kit and brought forth an aerosol can of mustard gas.

After every tiny, unsuspecting germ in my office and for fifteen square miles around had breathed its last, she strapped on what looked like a pair of bulletproof welder's goggles and started to explore the typewriter keyboard. Searching for a letter. *Any letter* which might seem familiar. She found some and this made her coo. Then she found a few others which she was almost sure she recognized as part of our language and she cooed some more.

All this cooing was unbalancing my metabolism so I tippy-toed out of the room and took the dogs for a walk, had lunch, and my daily siesta, then I tippy-toed back into my office. Most of the keyboard was still virgin territory so far as Miss Habbleburger was concerned. I felt then that she might be better suited for something else, so I asked her to stick a few stamps on some envelopes. This she did quite well—albeit by an extremely new method. She tore a stamp from its mother book, wet the back of her hand with her little gray tongue, dampened the stamp on her hand, and then pressed it onto the envelope. The whole process didn't take more than three or four minutes. Amazing.

The next one sent by The Cohen Girls came straight from the semifinals of the Harvest Moon Ball. She had eight-inch earrings that clanged with every piquant toss of her mink-dyed coiffure. She was barely able to manipulate her eyelids, they were so weighed down by her minesweeping false eyelashes, which were beaded with eight or more ounces of black-lead mascara. Little flecks of gold brightened her deep-purple eye shadow. Her hot gypsy eyes flashed hidden promises of a midnight rendezvous, if I didn't play my cards right. I looked at her hands and I knew right away they had never seen a sink full of dirty dishes. Or washed diapers. Or cleaned floors. Dug a little coal? Maybe. She was wearing so many huge and bizarre rings I thought at first that she had six fingers. I asked her how come she had so many rings, and she said she had belonged to a Lonely Hearts Club since she was thirteen. She also said she couldn't type because she was letting her nails grow, so when I said she wouldn't do, she asked for a letter of recommendation, so I put her in touch with Gorki Vassiloff of the Russian U.N. mission on 67th Street in New York—his brother is captain of a trawler.

Secretaries, typists, stenos, or whatever they are supposed to be, came and went with an ever-increasing velocity. Just when I felt that The Cohen Girls couldn't find anybody any worse than the last one—

they did. It was uncanny. I had never realized that America had such a vast untapped trained reserve of totally incompetent numps. I kept seeing those television commercials: "Hire the Handicapped!" I suddenly realized they weren't talking about the physically handicapped at all. They meant The Cohen Girls. *All* of them!

There was something about The Cohen Girl agency which I thought was commendable. In New York when we lived in an apartment, none of the outfits specializing in part-time office help would allow any of *their* girls to come to my *apartment*. It wasn't that they thought I was Rudolph the Red-nosed Raper, it was just "policy." When I explained that it was much easier to bend a girl over a desk in an *office*, where her screams would be ignored (or maybe taped—to be played back later at the Christmas party) this moved them not one little bit. They always made me feel as if I had called a nunnery and requested a few broads for King Farouk's birthday.

Secretaries—or lack of them—are not the only problems of wooing the muse in Outer Suburbia. A very large stumbling block to continued effort at my forty-year old Model Five Remington are the ordinary incidents I would escape if I owned an attaché case and could leave for the big city on the 7:38 with the rest of the chaps in the morning and return on the 5:09 at night. This way I would miss having Bobby and three or four small boys burning a small girl at the stake in one corner of my very limited workroom. This is not conducive to concentration, and a barbecue, no matter if it *is* Joan of Arc, I feel should be conducted in the open air.

Religious sects are continually beating a path to my door. They seem to think that I am ready to give up my F. Scott Fitzgerald way of life and wander about the countryside in sackcloth and sandals—spreading the word. They never tell me *which* word because it's in the pamphlet which they are selling for ten cents. Actually, most of these religious nuts don't want me to join at all—they want me to *give*. They want me to give them a small or large check to enable them to carry on their work. I ask, "What kind of work is it you do?" and they say, "We help bring God to the poor." Then I say, "I think it would be cheaper to bring the poor to God and it would make a nice outing for them. What do you think of that idea?" At about this point they begin to shuffle their feet and look at each other. (They travel in pairs like cautious cops.)

"Don't you care what happens to the poor?" says the male tubercular-looking one.

"Of course I do," I say, "but they have to be Indians."

"What?" says the female, who looks as though she's just been rejected by a body-snatching ring.

"Indians. *Poor* Indians. I think they should be helped and encouraged."

"Encouraged? Encouraged to do what?"

"Picket."

"I think we'd better go, Sister Amantha," says the tubercular one to the zombie.

"Why?" I say. "Why don't you come in and have a glass of blood? We just sacrificed a goat. Come on in, there's plenty for everybody. And we have jelly doughnuts."

This usually does it. First they edge away slowly, not daring to take their eyes off me or the Sacred Eagle perched on my gloved right hand. Then suddenly they panic and run screaming down the driveway, leaving a trail of gaudy leaflets that explain why God is better than a new color television set with remote-control tuning.

I really don't mind these interruptions because they allow me to leave my molehill of work and my mountain of blank white paper. The only trouble with door-to-door people is that they are apt to be stereotyped.

There's *always* the moron who, if he sells just two more subscriptions to the *Ladies' Home Journal*, will win a free trip to Philadelphia. When he first comes to the door he asks: "Mr. Merde?" which is the name I have on our mailbox—"Jos. Merde." I always reply, "Junior or Senior?" They ignore this or just don't hear it and launch into their overrehearsed hard sell: "Mr. Merde, one of your neighbors has been kind enough to give us your name." Then I say, "That's strange. We don't know our neighbors yet. We just moved in today." Then they say, "Mr. Merde, one of your neighbors has been kind enough to give us your name."

There are many other Outer Suburbia interruptions for an at-home worker. Veterans covered with army and navy store medals peddle poppies on almost any day except Poppy Day. Usually they have one empty sleeve pinned to their shoulder. One regular hero sometimes switches empty sleeves, and I show my extreme class by not calling this to his attention. This veteran of the war on poverty also visits Herb Cameron, who has no qualms about embarrassing this hustler, and when he mentioned the fact that the one-armed man couldn't seem to make up his mind about which arm was missing, this five-star poppy peddler agreed with Herb and admitted not being very well organized, because he was just starting out and he couldn't afford a dresser.

When I first moved to Old New Litchridge, I requested a shipyard in Stamford to send me a yacht catalog—just to find out what it had to offer and how much. It had plenty to offer and it's expensive. After I received the catalog and drooled over it, I thought this would be the end of it. I didn't spoil my record of being wrong. The next day a yacht salesman was at my front door. I hadn't realized we were so close. From Stamford, someone so intentioned could spit on Old New Litchridge. (Which may explain some of the eternal dampness.)

The yacht salesman had a smile that went clear around his head. He thought he had a live one. "Mr. Douglas?" he said.

"No," I said, with unprecedented caution. "He went back to Nome."

"Oh," said the salesman, his smile drooping to half-mast, then quickly recovering and remembering the mailbox, "Are you Mr. Merde?"

"Junior or Senior?" I said.

"Well, I guess—*Senior*," he said, holding up a model of the yacht he was selling.

"You want Junior," I said. "He's crazy about boats. We've got a whole bathtub full of them."

"But," said the yacht salesman, "this isn't for the bathtub. This is for the ocean. It's very seaworthy. You could sail it to Europe if you wanted to."

"Junior's only six years old," I said. "We wouldn't want him to try anything like that. Besides he'd miss too much school."

"You're making it tough for me," said the yacht salesman. "I'm just trying to sell yachts and you're making it tough for me."

"I'm sorry," I said, "but I didn't want a yacht. I just wanted the catalog."

"Oh," he said, taking off his black Captain Kidd eyepatch and dabbing his eyes with a handkerchief. "Gee, I just *gotta* sell a yacht sometime this year or I'll be back with the Hoover company."

"You mean selling vacuum cleaners?" I said.

"No," he said, "buttons—Hoover buttons."

"You're kidding."

"No, I'm not," he said. "You'd be surprised how many diehards they got left in New Canaan." (New Canaan is a town near Old New Litchridge where the Cabots speak only to the Lodges and the Lodges speak only to Merrill Lynch, Pierce, Fenner & Joe Bananas.)

The "Welcome Wagon Lady" is always good for an interruption. She welcomes us to Old New Litchridge about once very three months. She's very absentminded and evidently doesn't have any secret marking on the front gate like hobos used in the old days when railroads were carrying passengers and the hobos used to beg a handout from door to door, and the people who didn't give were marked lousy on the gate. The Welcome Wagon Lady, I think, should have had—for want of nothing better—this kind of system.

She always comes with a basket full of goodies like a free car wash with every Rolls-Royce you buy at Hugo's Used Rolls Lot. A free ticket to a kiddies' matinee at the Old New Litchridge movie house—good only when *The Creature from the Black Lagoon* is showing, which isn't too bad a deal because it's showing every Saturday afternoon. Kids are really loyal. Other gifts from The Lady Bountiful of the Old New Litchridge Store Owners Mafia include three cakes of Lava Soap in case Camay makes your hands rough. A free mole trap with a practice mole. And many other free gifts too frivolous to mention. After a while the Welcome Wagon Lady started welcoming us to Old New Litchridge a little too often. She dressed something like Little Red Riding Hood, so I didn't feed our wolf for a couple of days when I knew she was due, but Tanuki was conditioned to Alpo and wouldn't eat anything that didn't come in a can. This gave me a thought, but before I did anything, I borrowed a Connecticut law book, and, sure enough, there is a law against putting a lid on Welcome Wagon Ladies.

The poor thing doesn't come around anymore because she lost her job. In her enthusiasm to welcome what she thought was a newcomer, she gave *herself* away—to a member of the Old New Litchridge vice squad. It wasn't *fun*, so he decided it was *vice*.

Most of the interruptions that stem from living in Outer Suburbia and working at home come from myself. There's always something that needs attending to—like wandering around our vast two acres inspecting dead trees. Trees that have died from loneliness. They have no birds to fuss over them because the birds won't fuss over any tree that doesn't have bugs, and we have killed all the bugs by spraying them. Trees look at God all day and reach their leafy arms to pray—for bugs. And what do we give them? DDT with menthol.

Sometimes I take Bobby and we look for dinosaur tracks. This isn't as nutty as it sounds, because a hundred million or so years ago dinosaurs wandered all over Old New Litchridge. In fact, the New Haven Railroad is built on an old dinosaur trail. It's gotta be.

At other times when I get bored with staring at an unproductive typewriter that just sits there and sneers when I'm trying to be friendly, I play Fish-and-Game Warden. Whenever I see a weak-looking old man fishing in the pond across the road, I put on my puttees and my leather jacket and my Smokey the Bear hat and sneak up on him. If he doesn't drop dead when I step out from the bushes surrounding the pond, I say, "Let's see your fishing license." If the frail old man has a fishing license, I look to see if it's expired. If it hasn't, I give it back to him and say, "Well, everything seems to be in order, but don't forget—no fishing with an artificial light of any kind." At high noon this doesn't really shake anybody up too much, but it gives me an exit line while disappearing back into the bushes.

Once I caught a guy at high noon who *was* using an artificial light. I said, "What the hell is going on here?" And he said, "Screw, bum—I'm tryna find my contact lenses." He wasn't a frail old man, so I did as he suggested. I screwed right back to my unfriendly typewriter. It was unfriendly but it wasn't belligerent.

Always in Outer Suburbia there is something that needs fixing. At our house it's usually the clothes dryer. If you put too much in it, it coughs up the excess all over the floor, or it just stops dead and refuses to revolve unless the work load is reduced. Finally, after five years, we've found the correct amount which the dryer will handle without rebelling—two pair of Jockey shorts, or three handkerchiefs, or one-half of a sleeveless sports shirt. That's *it*. Poor Reiko spends most of her life these days sewing my sport shirts back together. Sometimes the poor thing gets mixed up and I get a shirt with two right sides. Rather than embarrass her, I wear it anyway and walk sideways like a spastic crab.

In the summer the power lawn mower won't start, and in the winter it turns into a snowblower that won't start. We are thinking of just having it bronzed and giving it to the Museum of Modern Art and calling it "Inertia" or maybe by its true name: "Goddamn sonofabitchin' goddamn machine."

This gem of modern technology is always good for a three- or four-hour happy interruption of my rigidly disciplined work schedule. I seem to be, sadly, just like every writer I know. We complain endlessly that there is never enough time to work, but the slightest *excuse*, like arrival of the new *Boys' Life* in the mail, or watching a raccoon trying to drown a pushy airedale in the pond, or a large helicopter flying overhead on the way to a new construction site, dangling an octette of portable privies (I always trustfully assume they are unoccupied), to knock off is most welcome, and if we live right we can stall around until it's really too late to work anymore that day.

Mice are, I guess, my principal source of interruptive excuses. I respect life, any kind of life, so much that I will not kill a mouse. Or anything. Flies that wander into the house are caught and helped back outside and freed again. Or any other bug or insect (if there's a difference) is treated the same way. I do not feel this strongly about people, so this gives me reason to believe that I cannot be entirely wrong.

Incidentally, there are only two animals that kill just for the hell of it—or the fun of it—rats and man. But let us get back to mice. And if you live in Outer Suburbia, you have them. Thousands upon thousands of them. There is no way to keep them out of your house, so you must learn to live with them. And I have. Every morning I visit my trapline of Hava-Hart traps, which catch them without injury, and take them outside in the yard and release them. I did this for a year or more without seemingly reducing the mouse population at all in our kitchen. I thought maybe the same mice were coming back, so I started marking their backs with bright yellow paint. Soon after I started doing this, my early-morning collection of captured mice contained a few mice that had their backs marked with paint—but not yellow. These mice backs were painted bright red, bright white, and bright blue. What the hell is this, I thought, as I repainted their backs with bright yellow, then took them outside and set them free.

Day by day the number of red, white, and blue painted mice increased until that was all that I found in my traps. There were no yellows at all. And the mice seemed to be enjoying a population explosion. I needed more Hava-Hart traps.

I met Herb Cameron in the hardware store. *He* had an armload of Hava-Hart traps. "Mice," he explained. "Pretty weird."

I said, "What do you mean, weird?"

"All the mice I catch are painted yellow on the back—I can't understand it."

"That *is* weird," I said.

"Yeah," he said. "I paint 'em red, white, and blue."

chapter 18

STATUS SEEMS TO BE MORE VIRULENTLY important in Outer Suburbia. And the symbols of it are strange indeed. The big status symbol in Old New Litchridge is a pond.

It doesn't have to be a *big* pond or a very *wet* pond, but it *must* attract wildfowl so you can let drop at cocktail parties, "Cost me three hundred and seventy-six dollars in bird food last winter."

We are "in" status-wise. We have a pond. But *no* wildfowl. So we're really "out." All we have is a rat. It's a water rat. It's also a recluse or else somebody swiped his Right Guard because we never see him with any other rat. We've seen him with a turtle a couple of times, but this seems to be a passing thing. A brief summer interlude. The whole situation makes it tough for us at social gatherings. Everyone else is chattering gaily away about Canada geese, mallards, trumpeter swans, and lovely lavender cranes. Once in a while someone turns and says, "Jack, you've got a pond." So that I don't have to mention our waterfowl shortage, I say, "You bet your ass we have." This sounds very unfriendly, especially if you happen to say it to an overripe dowager who frowns on gambling.

Of course there are our friends who always ask during a lull, "Hey, Jack, how's your rat?" Actually I don't think they really *want* to know. Because they ask it in the same tone you'd say, "How's your jungle rot these rainy days?" The whole attitude about our rat has put me on the defensive—so much so that I'm not only not ashamed that all we have in our pond is a rat, I'm swinging around to where I'm defensively *proud* of it, the way a father might act if his son had just been graduated from Harvard and still had difficulty in waving bye-bye. Who cares if he can't wave bye-bye, so long as he's got his law degree? That's the way I feel about our rat. He may not have been much of a rat, but he was ours. Every morning and every evening I left a little dish of cracked corn next to the pond. He ate every bit of it, then sat back on his haunches and stared pitifully at the back door—waiting for seconds. But no matter how wistful and all alone he'd look, I was firm. I didn't want our rat to gain too much weight. I didn't want people yelling across a crowded room on some enchanted Old New Litchridge evening, "Hey, Jack, how's your fat rat?"

Another status symbol up here in the other side of Paradise is the station wagon. Not how wide or how long or how expensive, but how dirty. That's what counts. Some social climbers, of course, cheat. They leave their wagons outside all winter and only drive them when roads are mud puddly enough to warrant it. These dreamers can never hope to achieve artificially what years of careful neglect can do naturally. A properly dirty station wagon cannot be faked. It must happen ecologically like the Rocky Mountains —or the Grand Canyon—or Princess Radziwill.

Tree surgery, and the amount of it you have done on your place, can also put you right up there in the status parade. Old New Litchridge is the convention city of the bug and insect world. Or so we are told by the George H. Burlingame tree surgery people. Mr. Burlingame is a man who didn't make it in dentistry so he has devoted his life to filling tree cavities. If Mr. Burlingame had his way, there wouldn't be an owl or a raccoon in all of Fairfield County. There would be no place for them to sleep. Whenever Mr. Burlingame sees a hole, he plugs it up with cement. His zeal along this line has not endeared him to everybody. He found this out the hard way when he was examined by Dr. Emerson, the hemorrhoid specialist, who *loves* raccoons and owls.

In Old New Litchridge tree surgery there is no such thing as a simple amputation by a man on a ladder with a saw on the end of a pole. When Mr. Burlingame arrives on the scene, he brings a complete staff and a portable operating theater on the end of a huge hinged steel leg. This leg lifts the operating theater eighty feet in the air like a Japanese juggler balancing a ball on his toe. In no time at all the amputations are completed, a bottle of sap plasma attached near the wounds with a spiked needle, and the tree owner is left with two round-the-clock registered tree nurses and a bill for $75. "What about penicillin?" the distraught dying elm owner shouts after the retreating Angel of Mercy. "Can't take a chance," shouts back Mr. Burlingame. "Might be allergic!"

Mr. Burlingame's services have become, without his knowledge, a status symbol. The more money you pay him for his arboreal succor, the higher your position in the Old New Litchridge caste system. And you can spend a fortune. *Spraying* alone could wipe out your life savings. Later on. Mr. Burlingame himself went bankrupt and all because he was converted to Christian Science and refused to believe in aphids. Gradually he went a little odd and now spends most of his time sitting by the side of the road, reading Mary Baker Eddy to a long-dead sycamore.

Everything in Outer Suburbia is euphemistically named. Garbage cans come in styles labeled "The Fiesta!" and "Mardi Gras!" and "Carnival!" and are painted in bright party colors. We have all three, and while they are colorful and gay, there has been a backlash. Every morning at 6:00 A.M., Julio, the garbage man, is given to shouting "Ole!" as he heaves each one of them onto his truck.

Once, when Reiko and Bobby were away on a visit to Japan, I climbed up on the roof above the garbage pail stand. It was cold because all I had on were my lacy Bill Blass pajamas (with the tiny jingle bells sewn on the fly). I waited until Julio arrived and started with his "Oles," then I suddenly showered him with colored streamers, confetti, and a few cherry bombs.

Julio stopped his heaving, spat some confetti out of his mouth, brushed some streamers off his shoulders, and said, "Hey, Señor Douglas, you're up on the roof early today." Then he yelled an extra "Ole," took the ladder I had used to get up to the roof, and removed it. Then he jumped into his truck and waved, "Have a good day," and zoomed off. Just as it started to hail.

There's something else we have here in Old New Litchridge, which for want of a better designation we call "The Mysterious Couple." These are people who live in the community, but are not part of it. No one knows anything about them, but rumors. And the rumors are fantastic.

We have just such a couple quite near us. Mr. and Mrs. John Hawkins. They live in a split-level, two-bedroom house which they call "Camelot," which should tell us something. Apparently every Saturday night they have "Jousting Parties" to which so far none of the local people have been invited. This should tell us something else. But it doesn't. I looked up "jousting" in Bennet Cerf's fifty-pound dictionary and it has no double meaning. It isn't even a pun. So what the hell are they doing in there every Saturday night with all the shades pulled down and Old English madrigals blasting away for hours? I got a small clue early one Sunday morning when I was walking my dogs. As I crossed the field in back of the Hawkins' place, I bumped into Mr. Hawkins. He was very busy burying something that looked like Lady Guinevere and Robert Goulet. When he saw me, he said, "Oh—hello—we watch you and your wife all the time on television. She's really cute—and funny, too." Then he went back to his digging.

Actually—thinking about it—in comparison to some of the other mysterious couples here in Old

New Litchridge, the Hawkinses are just plain ordinary everyday folks.

There is no mystery or euphemism connected with the taxes in Old New Litchridge. They are called "taxes," and they have been increased about 20 percent this year because we think we are about to be blessed with a new high school.

Mrs. Charleston Pyke, who is eighty-three years old and very wealthy, graciously donated three valuable acres of land to the town of Old New Litchridge—provided this land would be used for a new high school that will be needed to take care of the overflow of new students about seven years from now.

The three acres graciously donated by dear Mrs. Pyke are not quite large enough for a new high school, so dear Mrs. Pyke graciously agreed to sell the town 147 more acres, which just happened to adjoin the three acres she had so graciously donated in the first place. The price of this additional 147 acres, dear Mrs. Pyke graciously informed the town, was one million five hundred thousand dollars. Overnight our taxes went up 20 percent.

But this was only the beginning. After hundreds of meetings and consultations and concessions, eight million dollars was allotted for the new high school. High-priced *cost estimators* were brought in and informed that the town of Old New Litchridge had allotted eight million dollars for a new high school and it was now up to the *cost estimators* to *estimate* how much it would *cost*. After many many months of estimating, they estimated *eight million dollars*. For which they charged the town of Old New Litchridge an estimating cost (which was a percentage of the cost of the project) of three million dollars.

Town meetings were hurriedly called. There were only *five* million dollars left to pay for a high school that had been expertly estimated to cost *eight* million. Old New Litchridge had to face it—there must be revisions. Again the high-priced cost estimators were called in. Months went by and *finally* they managed to scale everything down so now the new high school would only cost *five* million dollars. Due to the extra complications resulting from the scaling down of the original figure, the price cost estimators had to put in many extra hours, so their fee for this second price cost revision was *two* million dollars. This left exactly *three* million dollars for the new high school.

The very prominent firm of architects, who have lavish offices in the Summit Hotel, and who had drawn the plans for the original eight-million-dollar high school, felt it beneath its dignity to revise its masterpiece downward to fit a far less munificent budget. Besides, the architects were very busy at the moment redesigning Nevada for Howard Hughes. (He's going to put an astrodome over the whole thing.) The architects collected their one-and-a-half-million-dollar fee and left for the West.

This left *one* million five hundred thousand dollars for the new high school, which is exactly what Old New Litchridge owes dear gracious Mrs. Pyke for the 147 acres it bought from her—plus, of course, 6¾ percent interest that had accumulated during the estimating.

We don't have town meetings anymore in Old New Litchridge. All the fun has gone out of them.

The schools we have now in Old New Litchridge are excellent. The teachers are all armed and the children are frisked twice a day. Bobby goes to kindergarten and he is in love with it. Every day he brings home three or four sheets of dirty shredded paper which he says is his homework. And maybe it is. Maybe it's a new profession he's learning. Dirty paper shredding. That doesn't sound too bad: "My son, the Dirty Paper Shredder." And I imagine if you plan this as a career you can't start too young.

The school bus, the cradle of champions, is something else again. The school bus driver wears a flak jacket and an ironworker's helmet, and the average length of time the school bus drivers put in is one hundred missions. After this they are sent to a rest and recreation area. Some, of course, crack after the first ten. They are sent to Moondog Hill, a local funny farm where they learn to weave baskets and become useful welfare cases.

The Old New Litchridge schools are long on artistic endeavor, from kindergarten on. Especially in the drama department. And they don't do *Snow White and the Seven Dwarfs* or *Tinker Bell and the Brownies.* None of that.

Bobby's first kindergarten play was *Death of a Salesman,* followed by *The Iceman Cometh.* Followed by one of Eugene O'Neill's unfinished plays. An unfinished play, incidentally, which Mr. O'Neill had ordered destroyed upon his death. I find it hard to understand why this particular unfinished play wasn't destroyed, because *all* Mr. O'Neill had written was "Act I, Scene 1." (Elliott Martin, a producer friend, tried to get it on, but was thwarted by Mike Nichols' refusal to direct it. Mr. Nichols' unerring dramaturgical instinct felt it needed work.)

Supposedly, the very early mornings in Outer Suburbia are quiet and peaceful and one can stroll out into one's garden and listen to the sound of one's birds. Somehow it doesn't work out this way. In the five years we've lived in Old New Litchridge, I haven't heard one goddamn bird. Not early in the morning or at any other time. I've heard power lawn mowers, power leaf blowers, power saws, and every other machine that can be run by an unmuffled two-cylinder gasoline engine at full throttle.

The noise from these things plus the intermittent voice of doom from the Czarina next door has caused Tanuki to spend most of the day cowering in his bomb shelter, and the latest report from the Audubon Society says, that the birds here no longer attempt to sing. For the past few years they have been just "mouthing" their songs. Like a nonsinging starlet in a musical movie.

I thought I had become used to everything which Old New Litchridge had to offer in the way of nerve-grinding noise, but I was wrong. Early one rainy April morning I was patrolling my garden—building roadblocks and placing "Keep Out" signs at all mole hole entrances and exits. Every once in a while, much to the puzzlement of God, who was watching me, I would bend over and yell down a mole hole: "Now hear this!" Then I would explain that, although some of my best friends were moles, Old New Litchridge was a restricted community, and if they wanted to eat tulip bulbs and heave up lawns, they would have to go over to the next town where moles were welcome so long as they weren't Jewish. This kind of nutty behavior didn't have any effect on the moles, but it sure made God think twice about having created me in His image. This last is what Pope John told me years ago in Rome when I told him that I had contracted a severe case of the trots from being last in line to kiss Father Gonzales' ring during High Mass in the Mexico City Cathedral.

After telling the moles I was only having fun with them, I sat down on something that used to be lawn furniture and sipped my morning coffee and watched the changing colors of the eastern sky. Suddenly World War III erupted in a patch of woods across the little river that separates Old New Litchridge and Stamford. Remembering the Continental Insurance Company's ad in *Life* magazine, I rushed inside the house, grabbed my three-cornered hat, and tore my old squirrel rifle from the wall over the fireplace. Reiko said, "What's the matter, Jacksan—squirrels?" I didn't answer her. There was no time. I didn't know what it was but I was ready to defend our two acres to the last mole.

As I tore off in the direction of the river and the now unbelievable sound of fury and rifle fire, I began to hear machine-gun bursts, and what sounded to me like (from watching news broadcasts) an occasional mortar. And an occasional mortar is plenty, considering the price of real estate around here. I didn't believe it possible, but suddenly the whole barrage escalated to an even more terrifying pitch. As I ran toward the sound, it got louder and louder, which was logical—now that I think back. What I was going to do when I got to where the battle was raging, I hadn't the slightest idea. Me, with one lousy single-shot Davy Crockett model squirrel rifle that had to be loaded from the front end, against a well-trained army. I stopped, and just before I started to sprint back to safety, I did a perverse thing. I put a lead ball into the front end of my riflle barrel, poured some black powder into the firing pan, pointed it toward the sky, and pulled the trigger. Jesus Christ what an explosion! Squirrel rifle! This damn thing would stop the battleship *Missouri!*

There was a brief pause from the invaders; the shooting ceased. Then, to borrow a phrase from a Fire Island weekend travel folder, all hell broke loose!

Whoever was in those woods let go with a barrage in my direction and pinned me down screaming for five minutes. I was being zapped, zunked, and zooked! And I was panic-stricken. I remembered a scene from an old Paul Muni movie where he jumped into a river to hide from the bloodhounds and breathed through a straw in his mouth, so I tried it. Unfortunately the river was only six inches deep and the straw I picked had a beetle inside it. One deep breath and instantly the beetle and I were both fighting for our lives. The beetle lost, but not before he grabbed everything that was grabbable on the way down. That wasn't too bad, but the trip back up was murder. I was never so glad to say good-bye to a beetle in my life.

As I lay there panting in the shallow river, glad to be alive, I suddenly had company. I was surrounded by the worst-looking group of cutthroats I had ever seen outside a Walt Disney movie. Each one was carrying a rifle or a machine gun and a holstered pistol. This is no ordinary bird-watching group, was the first thought that crossed my mind.

"What the hell do you think you're doing?" asked an evil-eyed, no-foreheaded gorilla who seemed to be in charge. He was pointing a rocket launcher right at my head. I was speechless temporarily. Then in a moment of sheer inspiration, I indicated the river I was lying in and said, "I was looking for my fish. He didn't come home last night." This prompted a brief whispered conference among my captors.

"Describe your fish," said one efficient-looking young man, taking a notebook and pencil from his inside coat pocket.

"Well," I said, fumbling, "he's not very tall and he has—"

That was as far as he let me get.

"What was he wearing?"

"This is ridiculous!" I said. "What could a fish be wearing?"

"It's *your* story," said the efficient-looking man. "Now, what was he wearing?"

Suddenly the gang started laughing. At the same time I saw the glint of a police badge.

"You're cops," I said hopefully.

"We're police officers," said the gorilla.

"Oh," I said, standing up and shaking the river out of my crotch. "What was all the shooting?"

"We're practicing—in case there's a riot this summer."

"A *riot* in Fairfield County?"

"Yeah, lot of tension along the shore. Too goddamn many yachts and not enough marinas. The whole thing is a tinderbox."

"I never thought of that," I said.

"You're just like the rest of them," said the gorilla. "Smug—complacent."

"I'm sorry," I said. "I'll become a Big Brother first thing tomorrow morning."

"Become a Big Sister and you'll get more action,"

said another cop who was carrying a sawed-off shotgun and a beaded bag.

"Quiet, Bonnie," said the gorilla.

That's about the extent of the *exciting* side of our stay in Outer Suburbia. There are so many exciting things that *didn't* happen. For example, one morning when I was home all alone, the telephone rang. It was the girl next door. She's about sixteen years old, very pretty, and she was breathing heavily. With this, I started to pant a little myself.

"Mr. Douglas," she said, "I *need* you! I can't put out the *fire! Hurry!!!*"

Jesus Christ, I thought, *this* is what they mean by the *now* generation!

"I'll be right over!" I shouted. And after a shot of Command hair spray, I started to run down the hill, changing into a clean bowling shirt en route. When I got there, smoke was pouring out of the wide-open front door. I always felt this little doll was sultry but this—I thought—is *ridiculous!* I rushed into the house. "Sandra! Where are you?" The smoke was thick.

"Oh, I'm so glad you've come," she said, coming toward me through the smoke. She was wearing the tiniest of bikinis. "The oven is on fire! You've got to *do* something!"

"You mean while the oven is on fire?"

She laughed. "Come on, Mr. Douglas. Go home and get your fire extinguisher and put out the fire in the oven. I gotta get to the *beach!*"

After opening the white-hot door of the oven, losing my fingertips in the process, I gave the interior of the flaming oven a shot with my Handy-Dandy Red Devil Fire Extinguisher. The flames were immediately smothered but the rest of the kitchen was a mess from the fire-fighting foam, but mostly from the oily smoke.

The cute little bikinied pussycat thanked me with a *handshake*. I cried all the way home.

Later, when her parents arrived on the scene, they were extremely annoyed with me because I had dirtied up their kitchen with my filthy fire extinguisher.

I had to apologize for my carelessness and inconsideration, and last Christmas I presented them with a lovely brand-new fire extinguisher, which is guaranteed—if they have to use it—not to leave a mess. It's filled with gasoline.